COOKING WITH

SEEDS

COOKING WITH
SEEDS

100 DELICIOUS RECIPES FOR THE FOODS YOU LOVE, MADE WITH NATURE'S MOST NUTRIENT-DENSE INGREDIENTS

CHARLYNE MATTOX

Photographs by Arnold Finkelstein

Da Capo
LIFE
LONG

A Member of the Perseus Books Group

Designed by Megan Jones Design, www.meganjonesdesign.com
Set in 10 point Archer by Megan Jones Design

Library of Congress Cataloging-in-Publication Data

Mattox, Charlyne.
  Cooking with seeds : 100 delicious recipes for the foods you love, made with natures most nutrient-dense ingredients / Charlyne Mattox ; photographs by Arnold Finkelstein.
      pages cm
  "A Member of the Perseus Books Group."
  Includes bibliographical references and index.
  ISBN 978-0-7382-1827-4 (pbk.) — ISBN 978-0-7382-1828-1 (e-book) 1. Cooking (Seeds) I. Finkelstein, Arnold. II. Title.

  TX814.5.S44M38 2015
  641.6'56—dc23

                    2015016687

First Da Capo Press edition 2015

Published by Da Capo Press
A Member of the Perseus Books Group
www.dacapopress.com

Note: The information in this book is true and complete to the best of our knowledge. This book is intended only as an informative guide for those wishing to know more about health issues. In no way is this book intended to replace, countermand, or conflict with the advice given to you by your own physician. The ultimate decision concerning care should be made between you and your doctor. We strongly recommend you follow his or her advice. Information in this book is general and is offered with no guarantees on the part of the authors or Da Capo Press. The authors and publisher disclaim all liability in connection with the use of this book.

Da Capo Press books are available at special discounts for bulk purchases in the US by corporations, institutions, and other organizations. For more information, please contact the Special Markets Department at the Perseus Books Group, 2300 Chestnut Street, Suite 200, Philadelphia, PA, 19103, or call (800) 810-4145, ext. 5000, or e-mail special.markets@perseusbooks.com.

10 9 8 7 6 5 4 3 2 1

*To my parents—thank you for showing me the world
and all the amazing food it has to offer.*

CONTENTS

◄ *Buttery Sesame Cookies, page 34*

SUNFLOWER · 147

PUMPKIN · 179

STAPLES · 201

INTRODUCTION

THE BASIC BUILDING BLOCKS OF LIFE AND DELICIOUS DISHES

Seeds are the basis for two of the things I enjoy most in life: cooking and gardening. Sow a seed and a plant will grow, producing more seeds. And, in many cases, you can eat not only the plant and the fruit it bears, but also its seeds. Scoop them out from any winter squash—think pumpkin, Hubbard, or acorn—give them a good rinse, roast them with spices, oil, and salt, and then toss in a salad or simply gobble them up as a snack. Crush coriander seeds to release their fragrant oils, sprinkle on pork chops with a little salt and pepper, and grill. Scatter coriander seeds in the garden, and a cilantro plant will pop up. Let the plant go to seed, and it will shoot up a pretty flower that looks similar to Queen Anne's lace. Harvest the seeds and start the process all over again. Seeds truly are the building blocks of life—each perfect seed contains the makings of a new plant.

Although grains (like barley, *farro*, and quinoa) and beans (such as black beans and lentils) are technically seeds, the focus of this book is on oilseeds—specifically sesame, chia, hemp, flax, poppy, sunflower, and pumpkin. Oilseeds are primarily made up of oil rather than starch. They can be pressed for their rich and flavorful oil or eaten whole or ground.

Why did I start cooking with and eating seeds? As every cook knows, a good dish has a perfect balance of fat, acid, seasoning, and texture. For texture, I have often added nuts. And, while I still find cooking with nuts rewarding (there is certainly no shortage of them in

this book!), after having cooked professionally for years and developed hundreds of recipes, I was looking for a new set of flavors to work with, to get excited about, and to make a part of my repertoire. What provides the same benefits? Seeds! Their texture and flavor rival that of nuts, and their health benefits are even more concentrated.

Seeds offer an impressive versatility and range of preparations that make them a perfect fit for any meal of the day. Blend any one of the seven presented here with water to make a delicious cow's milk alternative that will perk up coffee and add an additional layer of nutty flavor to granola and oatmeal. Bake pumpkin, hemp, and sesame seeds with nuts and dried fruit in crackers that are perfect for an afternoon snack with a smear of peanut butter or for gracing a cheese board. Mix ground flax into meatballs or combine with pine nuts and herbs for a delicious topping on roasted cod. Use the natural thickening properties of chia to whisk up an eggless Caesar salad dressing.

Adding flavor and texture to dishes is just part of the benefit of cooking with seeds. In the past couple of decades, groundbreaking discoveries have been made on how what we eat and put in our bodies affects our health and well-being. Health professionals and scientists have done in-depth studies on the nutritional value and health benefits of a diverse range of foods. Perhaps not surprisingly, they have discovered what native peoples have known for millennia: Seeds are a true superfood! The high fiber content in flax seeds and the gel-like qualities of chia seeds help make one feel fuller longer, and the high protein content in poppy seeds and hemp seeds make them a great alternative protein source for those trying to eat less meat. Seeds not only contain large numbers of minerals and vitamins, they are also packed full of disease-fighting compounds. Sesame, for example, has been proven to help reduce aging-related ailments such as heart disease and cancer. And pumpkin seeds and their oils help reduce hypertension.

I do my best to eat a healthful diet but, like most, succumb to whims and cravings. (As I write this I am eating dark chocolate dipped in peanut butter!) While many of the recipes in this book are health conscious, just to be clear, this is not, strictly speaking, a "health book." Rather, it is one full of recipes that are incredibly enjoyable, and healthful food that is made even more so by the addition of seeds. Take, for example, a rich and creamy fennel and onion quiche with a fiber-rich flax seed crust (page 80) or thinly pounded chicken breasts that are coated in a copious amount of sesame seeds (page 27).

Preparing and sharing satisfying, delicious, and, in most cases, simple food forms the core of my cooking philosophy. I like to create recipes and prepare meals with memorable flavor and texture combinations; ones that I am proud to serve to my family and friends.

While some of the recipes require very little prep time and others take a bit longer, I've made sure that the steps for each are clear and concise so that no matter what your level of cooking skill, you can master these recipes.

The following seven chapters each focus on a different seed and feature recipes that highlight its flavor, texture, and appearance. Each chapter starts with a short introduction to the seed's unique flavor profile and health benefits and provides information on where and how to purchase and store them, as well as simple guidelines for toasting. In each chapter you will find recipes for seed milks, seed butters, smoothies, and snacks, as well as a plethora of main dishes and desserts.

So, stock up and get in the kitchen! In no time you will find ways to add a cup, a dash, or a sprinkle of seeds to everything you make.

KITCHEN BASICS

Most of the ingredients and equipment used in this book will be familiar to anyone with a moderate level of cooking acumen. More often than not, you'll have many of the basic ingredients on hand or you can purchase them at a standard market. Occasionally, though, you'll need to make a trip to a specialty grocer, so I've listed below brief primers on the specialty items under the "pantry" heading. Additionally, if you have a well-stocked kitchen, you should have all the equipment on hand to make any of these recipes. That said, under the "tools of the trade" section, I have outlined a few of the larger pieces of equipment that are used repeatedly, as well as a few less common items.

Lastly, I have included a quick tutorial on how to set up a grill. As a side note, if you don't have a grill (sorry, city dwellers—well, most of you anyway), unless otherwise instructed, you can use a grill pan placed on your stovetop to cook any of the grilling recipes.

PANTRY

Aleppo Pepper

A crushed and dried cherry-red pepper hailing from Syria and Turkey, Aleppo is moderately spicy, a little smoky, and just the slightest bit oily. Look for it in Middle Eastern and specialty markets.

Bonito Flakes

Known as *katsuobushi* in Japan, these pink shavings are made from dried and smoked pieces of bonito (a fish similar to tuna). They are an essential ingredient in Japanese cooking, and one of the main ingredients in the broth, dashi. Purchase at Asian or health-food markets.

Borlotti Beans

A member of the cranberry bean family, these speckled beans (they turn brownish red when cooked) have a thick skin and creamy interior. They are available canned or dried at specialty markets.

Buckwheat Flour

Made from ground buckwheat grains (a seed that is not related to wheat), it has a tan to gray color and a deep, robust flavor. While buckwheat is gluten-free, because of its strong taste, it is often mixed with other (gluten) flours in baking recipes. Look for it in health-food stores.

Crema

Not to be confused with the foamy goodness on the top of an espresso, this soured and thickened cream product is a staple in Mexican cooking. It is thinner than sour cream, yet has a similar tang. Look for it in Latin markets or in the specialty sections of your regular grocery store.

Dried Cornhusks

Dried cornhusks are simply the outer husks of corncobs that have been cleaned and dried. Although not edible, they are most commonly used as wrappings for tamales (well for culinary purposes, anyway—cornhusk crafts anyone?). Look for them in Latin markets or order a bag online.

Dried Mushrooms

Any number of mushrooms are available dried, and the style of cooking you are doing will determine which type you use. For Asian dishes, reach for dried shiitake (available in Asian markets); for French, Italian, or Latin dishes, try dried porcini (available everywhere).

Dutch-Processed Cocoa Powder

Dutching is the process of washing cocoa powder in a potassium solution. The end result is a darker powder, which is less acidic and has a more robust chocolate flavor than natural cocoa. It's available in most high-end grocery stores. Because of the change in alkalinity (which can affect how a baked good rises, among other things), in most recipes it is ill advised to substitute Dutch processed for natural cocoa powder. That said, I have designed all the recipes in this book to work with both, though Dutch processed is my preference.

Guanciale

Guanciale, which means "pillow" in Italian, is an aged pork product that is made by rubbing a pork jowl with salt, sugar, and spices and then curing it for approximately three to four weeks. It has a higher fat-to-meat ratio and stronger flavor than pancetta. Look for it in specialty markets.

Kombu

A thick and dark green seaweed that is available dried, in sheets, in all Asian markets and in health-food stores. It is another one of the main ingredients in dashi.

Labneh

This Lebanese spread is made by draining full-fat Greek yogurt. It has a thick texture and an extra-tangy flavor. Look for tubs of it in specialty grocery stores or make your own by straining yogurt overnight in the refrigerator.

Masa Harina

Masa harina is the dried and powdered version of Mexican corn dough called *masa de maize* (*masa* means "dough" in Spanish). It's used to make tortillas, tamales, and arepas, among other things. Look for five-pound bags in Latin markets; reconstitute with water before using.

Mirin

Mirin is a Japanese sweet cooking wine that is made by fermenting rice. The most common variety has a light golden color and a syrupy consistency. Because of its short fermentation period, it typically has a low level of alcohol. Look for it in specialty or Asian markets.

Nori

A thin seaweed that is dried and toasted after harvesting; in the US, nori is most commonly used as the wrapping for sushi rolls. Look for it in Asian markets. A special note about storage: Be sure to keep opened packages tightly sealed. Nori is very sensitive to humidity and loses its crispiness very quickly.

Pomegranate Molasses

Pomegranate molasses is pomegranate juice and sugar that have been cooked into a thick syrup. Look for bottles in Middle Eastern or specialty markets.

Queso Fresco

A semisoft cow's milk cheese that hails from Mexico. It's typically served shredded or crumbled and has a mild flavor. Look for it in Latin markets.

Rye Flour

Ground from dried rye grain, this flour has a sour taste and ranges in color from white to beige. Look for it in health-food markets.

Speck

Another cured pork product (I do love a good cured meat), speck is made by rubbing a boned ham leg with spices (a notable flavor is juniper berry), which is then cured, cold smoked, and dried. It has a smoky flavor and somewhat firm texture.

Tamarind

The fruit of the tamarind tree, these long pods are filled with an edible pulp that is a dark maroon color and has a sweet-sour flavor. Look for blocks of the pulp in specialty, Mexican, Indian, or Southeast Asian markets.

Tomatillos

A member of the nightshade family (eggplants, tomatoes, potatoes), tomatillos are small, round green fruits covered in a thin, inedible, papery husk. They have a slightly sour flavor and are a staple in Mexican cuisine. Look for them in Latin markets.

Za'atar

A Middle Eastern spice mix whose makeup can vary depending on where it hails from, but typically it involves a mixture of sumac, sesame seeds, and oregano, thyme, or marjoram. Look for it in specialty or Middle Eastern markets.

TOOLS OF THE TRADE

Blender

I consider myself very lucky to own a high-powered Vitamix, but I understand that buying one is not in everyone's budget, and it is certainly not 100 percent necessary for making any of the recipes in this book. If you have a less powerful blender, simply soak the seeds longer before processing the seed milks, finely chop the components for pesto, and add a little more liquid when making a smoothie. When I talk about the "feed tube" in a recipe, I'm referring to the hole in the lid of the blender (it typically has a plug of some sort). This hole allows you to feed oil or liquid into the blender while it's running without making an awful mess of your kitchen.

Bundt Pan

A Bundt pan is a deep, round pan with a column in the middle. It has a curved bottom and shaped sides (not to be confused with a removable, flat-bottomed, straight-sided angel food pan). Many people think of cakes cooked in Bundt pans as "church cakes" because there were always one or two on a church buffet spread when they were growing up. I really love them because their decorative shapes can make even a ho-hum-looking cake, fancy.

Candy/Deep-Fry Thermometer

This tool is invaluable for frying and candy making. It helps ensure that oil stays the perfect temperature for crispy and golden-brown fried chicken (350°F) or that you pull that bubbling sugar mixture off the stove at the exact right moment for extra-snappy seed brittle (300 to 310°F). To use, clip onto the side of a pan, and make sure the bottom bulb of the thermometer is submerged in the liquid.

Electric Mixer

In my opinion, an electric stand mixer is another kitchen must-have. Although a cheaper hand mixer works perfectly fine in many instances—whipping cream or egg whites—bigger, tougher jobs are easily tackled with a heavy-duty stand mixer. Use the dough hook to turn out a batch of rolls or the beater attachment to quickly mix a batch of cookies.

Food Processor

Another kitchen must. It's essential for making supersmooth dips and nut butters, and I love it for whipping up flaky pie dough. No need to go fancy (mine is at least fifteen years old and still kickin'), but I strongly believe it's worth investing in. (I also use a Cuisinart Mini Prep; it's not as essential, but I do love it for chopping nuts and cheese.)

Ice-Cream Machine

Although this machine may spend most of the year in the back of the cupboard, when summer rolls around, you will be so glad you own it because nothing compares to the soft, velvety texture of homemade ice cream. If you don't already have one, do a little research before purchasing. The cheaper ones (under $100) tend to either take a long time to freeze the ice cream or make it grainy.

Instant-Read Thermometer

Buy one of these, and it will be the best ten dollars you ever spent. Using a thermometer to take the internal temperature of meat is the only foolproof way to make sure those expensive cuts are cooked to perfection every time.

Kitchen Scale

Unless you plan on doing a lot of precision baking, a kitchen scale is not 100 percent necessary. When developing recipes, I use one to weigh ingredients and check portion sizes, but for the home cook, they are most useful for, and make quick work of, portioning dough (see Black Sesame Seed Dinner Rolls on page 17).

Microplane

Whatever did we do before Microplanes?! This supersharp, amazing grater is just the right tool for getting feathery wisps of Parmesan cheese and for finely grating citrus peel and ginger.

Nut Milk Bag

The key to good seed milk is a smooth, creamy texture that is free of as much of the pulp as possible, and a surefire way to get there is with a nut bag. It has very fine holes so it strains out most of the pulp, is neat and efficient, and is reusable (waste not, want not). If you plan to make a lot of seed (or nut) milks, it's essential.

Spice Grinder

Also known as an electric, whole bean coffee grinder. There are versions that are designed to just grind spices, but why not get one that does double duty?

Springform Pan

The spring refers to the latch on the side of the pan that one either tightens to attach the ring-like sleeve to the base of the pan (creating a tight seal) or loosens to release it. This is the pan you want to use if you are making something with a crust that you don't want to serve directly out of the pan (like the Caramelized Onion and Fennel Quiche with Flax-Speckled Crust, page 80) or a delicate cake that can't be turned out of its pan, like cheesecake.

Tortilla Press

Another very specific tool that may not get a lot of use but is invaluable when you just have to make a batch of fresh tortillas. Place a ball of dough between its two disks (which are attached with a hinge), press down on the attached handle, and voilà—a tortilla! One can be had online for around twenty dollars.

HOW TO SET UP A GRILL

For indirect grilling, you want to have the hot coals (or flames lit on a gas grill) only on one side of the grill so that you can set the food next to (not directly over) the heat source. This allows you to cook (and smoke) large pieces of meat. If you were to put big cuts directly over the heat source, the outside would burn before the interior had time to cook to the correct temperature. Use this setup when you are cooking a whole chicken, brisket, or pork shoulder. For direct grilling (good for smaller cuts like steaks and chops), set up the grill in the same way, but cook directly over the heat source. Leaving a cold side allows you to move the food if it starts to get too dark or burns.

SESAME

Originally from the African savanna, sesame is now grown in India, China, Mexico, and Texas. This very wide-ranging cultivation may help explain its universal appeal. In a well-known Japanese dish, sesame seeds are ground into a complex dressing with soy sauce and sugar and served with lightly wilted spinach. *Til ke ladoo* is a delicious Indian sweet made with copious amounts of sesame seeds, sugar, and spices. Sicilians bake up an airy semolina bread known as *pane Siciliano*, where the outside is entirely coated with these little gems. Heck, even my southern grandmas cooked with them (though they knew them as benne seeds)—caramel cake with a scoop of vanilla ice cream and a generous sprinkling of sesame seeds, anyone?

Sesame seeds are made up of 50 percent oil, which explains the origin of their name, a derivation of two ancient Middle Eastern words meaning "oil" and "plant." The seeds contain 25 percent protein and are full of many essential minerals, such as magnesium and calcium, as well as vitamin B1 and fiber. The oil contains high levels of antioxidant phenolic compounds and vitamin E, which helps make them resistant to rancidity and oxidation. Sesame oil is available either toasted or untoasted. The toasted variety is darker in color, with a roasted and smoky flavor. Untoasted oil is mild tasting with a light color, similar to canola oil.

TASTE, TEXTURE, APPEARANCE

These little beauties have a rich nutty flavor and pleasantly crunchy texture. White sesame seeds can be purchased hulled or unhulled. Unhulled seeds are golden-brown, and though they are higher in calcium than white (hulled) seeds, if used in large quantities, they impart a bitter flavor. Use either form in the following recipes unless it specifically calls for hulled. Black sesame seeds (they are always unhulled) have a firmer texture and a more peppery taste.

BUYING AND KEEPING

White sesame seeds are available packaged in most grocery stores, in bulk at health-food stores, and also online. Black sesame seeds can be a little harder to find; look for them in Asian markets or order a bag online. Store both varieties in a cool, dark place for three months, in the refrigerator for six months, or in the freezer for up to one year. Store sesame oil in the refrigerator for up to one year.

TOASTING INSTRUCTIONS

Toasting really highlights the flavor of sesame. Toast in a medium sauté pan over medium heat, stirring, until light golden-brown, in the case of white sesame seeds, and fragrant, 3 to 5 minutes, or in a 350°F oven, stirring once, 7 to 10 minutes. For best results, toast seeds just before using.

sesame milk

MAKES 3 CUPS

This is one of those recipes where you'll want to make sure to use hulled sesame seeds; unhulled seeds make a very bitter milk, no matter how much honey you add. Try this creamy milk in a mango sorbet float or in rice pudding with chopped pineapple. Store in an airtight container, in the refrigerator, for one week.

1 cup hulled white sesame seeds
4 pitted dates
1 tablespoon honey
Kosher salt

Place the sesame seeds in 3 cups of water. Soak overnight in the refrigerator; drain.

Place the sesame seeds, dates, honey, a pinch of salt, and 3 cups of water in a blender. Blend on high until very smooth, 2 to 3 minutes.

Strain the milk through a nut milk bag or a very fine mesh metal strainer. Chill completely.

double sesame fruit smoothie

MAKES 1 SERVING

This rich drink has a double dose of sesame: seeds and milk. If you don't have a batch of sesame milk on hand, use any type of milk or milk alternative. Feel free to substitute one cup of fresh sweet strawberries for the frozen; just be sure to add one-half cup of ice to chill the smoothie.

1 cup whole frozen strawberries
½ banana
½ cup Sesame Milk (page 13)
2 tablespoons toasted white sesame seeds
1 tablespoon agave

Place the strawberries, banana, sesame milk, sesame seeds, and agave in a blender. Blend on high until very smooth, 30 seconds.

tahini

MAKES ⅔ CUP

I always have tahini in my fridge. I often find it's just the thing I need to make dinner that much better. Stir a little into mayo for a decadent burger sauce and french fry dipper, or spread it onto toast and drizzle with honey for a quick snack. A staple in North African, Turkish, and Middle Eastern cuisine, tahini is simply ground sesame seeds and, in this case, a little olive oil. You can buy jars or cans of it in the market, but it's hard to guarantee freshness—and the homemade stuff truly is superior. Store in an airtight container, in the refrigerator, for one month.

2 cups toasted hulled white sesame seeds

3 tablespoons olive oil

Place the sesame seeds and oil in a food processor. Process, stopping the food processor and scraping down the bowl as necessary, until the tahini is smooth and creamy, 3 to 4 minutes.

Strain through a fine mesh sieve.

spicy herb and sesame sauce

MAKES ¾ CUP

The mixture of crunchy sesame seeds and sharp sherry vinegar makes this a perfect accompaniment for pan-seared fish or grilled flank steak. The Aleppo pepper adds a tiny bit of heat and a lot of complex tart and fruity pepper flavor. Look for it in specialty markets or online. Store, without the vinegar, in an airtight container, in the refrigerator, for up to one day. Stir in the vinegar just before serving.

1 packed cup fresh Italian parsley leaves, finely chopped

¼ cup packed fresh oregano leaves, finely chopped

2 tablespoons toasted white sesame seeds

1 small garlic clove, pressed

1 teaspoon Aleppo pepper

⅓ cup olive oil

4 teaspoons sherry vinegar

Kosher salt

Combine the parsley, oregano, sesame seeds, garlic, pepper, oil, and vinegar in a bowl. Season with salt.

sesame and salt shake

MAKES ¼ CUP

Also known as *gomasio*, this shake is versatile and wonderful to have on hand when a dish just needs a little extra salty, savory goodness. I love it on roasted vegetables or stir-fry or sprinkled on a soup. Store in an airtight container, at room temperature, for one month.

1 teaspoon flaky sea salt (such as Maldon)
5 tablespoons toasted white sesame seeds, divided

Place the salt and 4 tablespoons of the sesame seeds in a spice grinder. Pulse twice. Transfer to a bowl and stir in the remaining tablespoon of seeds.

miso sesame spread

MAKES 1 CUP

Building a perfect sandwich can be tough, and without the right spread, it's downright impossible. This all-purpose one is savory from the miso, tangy from the yogurt, and has a little kick from the mustard. It's great with sliced pork and sweet pickled cucumber sandwiches or the Chile Roasted Squash Wedges with Sesame and Pumpkin Seeds (page 22). To prevent clumps, mix the miso with a few tablespoons of the yogurt before combining it with the rest. Store in an airtight container, in the refrigerator, for one week.

¾ cup plain Greek yogurt
2 tablespoons Dijon mustard
1 tablespoon white miso
1 tablespoon toasted white sesame seeds
Freshly ground black pepper

Combine the yogurt, mustard, miso, and sesame seeds in a bowl. Season with pepper.

black sesame seed dinner rolls

Tender rolls studded with black sesame seeds are just the thing to serve with your next holiday meal. And if there are any leftover, they are great reheated with a smear of butter and orange marmalade. The dough is sticky, so work it into balls with well-floured hands. The formed balls can be frozen (before they rise) for up to two weeks. Defrost in the refrigerator, then allow to rise, at room temperature, until doubled in size, one to two hours.

¼ cup (½ stick), plus ½ cup (1 stick) unsalted butter, cut up, divided

¼ cup water, warmed to 100 to 110°F

¼ teaspoon sugar

1 package active dry yeast (¼ ounce)

1 cup whole milk, warmed slightly

3 cups all-purpose flour, spooned and leveled, plus more for the work surface

½ cup whole wheat flour, spooned and leveled

2 tablespoons black sesame seeds

1 tablespoon kosher salt

Flaky sea salt (such as Maldon), for sprinkling

Melt 1 tablespoon of the butter and rub the inside of a bowl with it.

Combine the water and sugar in a measuring cup. Sprinkle the yeast on top of the water. Let sit until the yeast is bubbling, 5 to 7 minutes. (If the yeast does not bubble, discard the mixture and start again.) Whisk in the milk.

Whisk together the flours, sesame seeds, and kosher salt in the bowl of an electric mixer. Add the yeast mixture and stir to combine. Start beating the mixture with a dough hook while adding the ½-cup cut-up butter, one piece at a time. Once all of the butter is added, continue to beat on high until the dough fully comes together, 6 to 8 minutes.

Transfer the dough to the buttered bowl and turn to coat with the butter. Cover the bowl with a dishtowel and place it in a warm (but not hot) place. Let the dough rise until doubled in size, 45 minutes to 1 hour.

Turn the dough out onto a floured work surface and knead, 8 to 10 times. Divide the dough into 12 equal-sized balls and place in a 3-quart baking dish, spacing evenly. Cover the baking dish with a dishtowel and place it in a warm (but not hot) place. Let rest until the rolls have doubled in size, 45 minutes to 1 hour.

Preheat oven to 400°F. Melt the remaining 3 tablespoons of butter and brush the top of the rolls. Lightly sprinkle the sea salt.

Bake until the rolls are golden-brown, 20 to 24 minutes.

Serve warm.

tropical fruit muesli

MAKES 6 CUPS

Muesli—a grain, nut, and dried-fruit cereal invented by a Swiss doctor—is great straight out of the bag over yogurt or with milk. You can also soak it overnight to create a cold, soft, porridge-like breakfast. I found that the perfect porridge proportions are two-thirds cup of muesli soaked with one-half cup of milk. The topper? Fresh fruit, naturally. An added bonus, it's a very versatile recipe. Does someone in your house have a peanut allergy? Simply substitute the nut of your choice. You can also go less tropical and switch out the fruit with dried cherries, dates, and figs. Store in an airtight container, at room temperature, for one month.

2 cups old-fashioned rolled oats

1 cup unsweetened coconut

1 cup roasted peanuts, very coarsely chopped

½ cup toasted hulled white sesame seeds

½ cup toasted pepitas

½ cup chopped dried mango

½ cup chopped dried pineapple

¼ cup chopped crystallized ginger

Milk or yogurt and fresh fruit, for serving

Preheat oven to 350°F.

Spread the oats on a large, rimmed baking sheet. Toast, stirring occasionally, until golden-brown and fragrant, 7 to 9 minutes. Spread the coconut on a small, rimmed baking sheet. Toast, stirring often, until golden-brown, 7 to 9 minutes. Cool completely.

Combine the toasted oats and coconut, peanuts, sesame seeds, pepitas, mango, pineapple, and ginger in a bowl.

Serve with milk or yogurt and topped with fresh fruit.

two-bean salad with fried capers

MAKES 4 SERVINGS

Tangy shallot, crispy fried capers, green beans, and borlotti beans (a variety of the cranberry bean that has a thick skin and creamy interior) provide a modern update to the classic three (well, in this case two) bean salad. Look for capers that are big and plump. When fried they will burst open slightly and have a nice meaty texture. If you have salt-packed capers, soak them in water for five to ten minutes to remove some of the excess salt.

1 medium shallot, thinly sliced

4 teaspoons red wine vinegar

Kosher salt and freshly ground black pepper

½ pound green beans, stem ends trimmed

2 tablespoons olive oil

3 tablespoons capers, drained and patted dry

1 cup cooked borlotti beans

1 tablespoon toasted white sesame seeds

Toss the shallot and vinegar in a bowl. Season with salt and pepper. Let sit, stirring occasionally, until the shallot is bright pink and slightly soft, 8 to 10 minutes.

Bring a large saucepan of salted water to a boil. Add the green beans and cook until tender, 2 to 4 minutes. Drain and run under cold water to cool completely. Shake to remove as much water as possible.

Cook the capers in the oil in a small sauté pan over medium-high heat, stirring occasionally, until crispy, 2 to 3 minutes.

Add the blanched green beans, fried capers and oil, borlotti beans, and sesame seeds to the bowl with the shallots. Season with salt and pepper.

sesame seed falafel salad
with tahini dressing

There is no better snack or quick, on-the-go lunch than falafel. The balls are not only filling but are chock-full of flavorful spices and herbs. In this recipe, they are served over a salad but feel free to wrap them up in a pita or tortilla. Falafel are best eaten within a half hour of being made since they lose their crispiness as they sit. The falafel mixture can be made up to one day ahead; store in an airtight container, in the refrigerator. The dressing can also be made ahead but will thicken as it sits; thin with a little water before serving.

½ cup bulgur

3 tablespoons tahini (store-bought or page 14)

2 tablespoons olive oil

2 tablespoons fresh lemon juice

Kosher salt and freshly ground black pepper

2 teaspoons cumin seeds

1 teaspoon coriander seeds

½ cup fresh Italian parsley leaves

¼ cup fresh cilantro leaves and tender stems

4 scallions, coarsely chopped

3 small garlic cloves

1 cup canned chickpeas, rinsed

1 teaspoon baking powder

¼ cup all-purpose flour, spooned and leveled

2 tablespoons toasted white sesame seeds

1 cup canola oil

1 bunch arugula

4 radishes, sliced

4 pieces flatbread, warmed

2 ounces feta, crumbled

Harissa (page 206) and cured olives, for serving

Cook the bulgur according the directions on the package. Spread the grains on a small baking sheet or plate and refrigerate, stirring once, until the grains are completely dry, 30 minutes.

Combine the tahini, olive oil, lemon juice, and 1 tablespoon water in a bowl. Season with salt and pepper.

Toast the cumin and coriander seeds in a small sauté pan over low heat until fragrant, 1 to 2 minutes. Finely grind in a spice grinder.

Place the parsley, cilantro, scallions, and garlic in a food processor. Process until finely chopped, 30 seconds to 1 minute. Add the ground spices, chickpeas, and baking powder. Process until the chickpeas are coarsely chopped, 10 to 20 seconds. Add the cooked bulgur, flour, and sesame seeds and pulse to combine. Use a 1-tablespoon cookie scoop or tablespoon measure to divide the mixture into balls. Gently press the balls to flatten into hockey-puck-shaped disks.

Heat the canola oil in a large, straight-sided sauté pan over medium-high heat (the oil should be about ½ inch deep). Fry the falafel, in 2 batches, turning once, until golden-brown, 6 to 8 minutes. Drain on paper towels.

Serve the falafel with the arugula, radishes, flatbread, feta, harissa, and olives, drizzled with the tahini dressing.

chile roasted squash wedges
with sesame and pumpkin seeds

MAKES 4 SERVINGS

These cover-worthy roasted squash wedges are loaded with two different seeds, spiced up with ginger and Fresno chiles, and jazzed up with a quick drizzle of rice vinegar. For dipping, serve with the Miso Sesame Spread (page 16). Dividing the squash between two trays gives them enough room to cook and pick up a little color, rather than just steam.

1 2-pound Hubbard squash, seeds discarded and cut into 1-inch wedges

2 tablespoons white sesame seeds

2 tablespoons canola oil

Kosher salt and freshly ground black pepper

2 red Fresno chiles, sliced

1 small piece fresh ginger, peeled and sliced

2 tablespoons unseasoned rice vinegar

2 tablespoons toasted pepitas

Preheat oven to 425°F.

Toss together the squash, sesame seeds, and oil. Season with salt and pepper. Divide between 2 rimmed baking sheets. Roast until the squash is starting to soften, 15 to 17 minutes. Remove the baking sheet from the oven. Turn the squash and add the chiles and ginger to the baking sheets. Return the baking sheets to the oven. Rotate the sheets front to back and top to bottom, and continue to roast until the squash is golden-brown and tender, 15 to 17 minutes. Drizzle with the rice vinegar.

Serve sprinkled with the pepitas.

scallops with black sesame seeds and lime

In our house, scallops are often requested, and this recipe in particular is always a hit. Rich buttery scallops are balanced with a sneaky bit of pepper from the sesame seeds and a hit of bright lime juice and zest. Covering the pan after you add the sesame seeds will prevent them from flying all over the kitchen. Serve these on their own as an appetizer or with steamed bok choy or spinach and jasmine rice for dinner.

½ tablespoon unsalted butter

½ tablespoon olive oil

8 diver scallops, tendon discarded and patted dry

Kosher salt and freshly ground black pepper

1 teaspoon black sesame seeds

½ teaspoon finely grated lime zest and 2 teaspoons lime juice, plus lime wedges for serving

Heat the butter and oil in a large nonstick sauté pan over medium-high heat until the butter is melted. Season the scallops with salt and pepper.

Cook the scallops on one side until golden-brown, 2 to 4 minutes. Flip and cook until just cooked through, 1 to 2 minutes more.

Transfer the scallops to a plate. Remove the skillet from the heat. Add the sesame seeds to the skillet and quickly cover with a lid. Keep the lid on the skillet until the seeds stop popping, about 30 seconds. Return the scallops (and any juices) to the skillet. Top with the lime zest and juice and turn to coat.

Serve the scallops immediately, drizzled with the juices from the pan and lime wedges alongside.

> **TIP** *True diver scallops are harvested by hand from the ocean floor. They can be quite expensive but are worth the cost for special occasions. The tough tendon (it holds the scallop to its shell) is a small rectangle of tissue attached to the side of the scallop. It is very easy to remove; simply peel it off.*

salmon-filled japanese rice balls

Wrap sticky short-grained rice around a filling, in this case roasted salmon, to make Japanese rice balls, aka onigiri. They are fun to assemble (it's a great way to get kids cooking!) and can be filled with myriad seafood and veggies (try a vegetarian version filled with cucumber and pickled ginger or avocado and wasabi). Look for sheets of nori (a paper-thin, dried, and toasted seaweed) in Asian markets or order it online. The balls can be formed up to one day ahead but don't wrap with the nori until just before serving; it loses its crispiness very quickly.

1 4-ounce skinless salmon fillet

Kosher salt and freshly ground black pepper

1 cup short-grain white rice

2 tablespoons toasted hulled white sesame seeds

1 piece nori, cut into 12 strips

Ponzu (page 205)

TIP *It's important that you keep your hands wet while forming the balls, otherwise the rice will stick to them and you will end up with a big mess.*

Preheat oven to 350°F.

Season the salmon with salt and pepper. Roast on a small baking sheet until just opaque throughout, 9 to 11 minutes. Cool to room temperature and then break into small flakes.

Place the rice in a colander and rinse, rubbing the grains together with your fingers, until the draining water is no longer cloudy. Shake vigorously to remove as much water as possible. Combine the rinsed rice and 1 cup plus 2 tablespoons water in a small saucepan. Season with salt. Bring to a boil. Cover the saucepan, reduce the heat to low, and gently simmer until the rice is tender, 14 to 16 minutes. Remove from the heat and let sit, covered, for 10 minutes. Stir the sesame seeds into the rice with a fork. Cool until able to handle.

Wet hands with cold water. Place ¼-cup rice in the palm of one hand and make a small dimple in the middle. Place 2 teaspoons of the salmon in the dimple and squeeze the rice over the salmon to enclose. Form the rice into a ball, squeezing to help the rice stick together. Wrap the ball in a strip of nori, dabbing the end with a little water to help it adhere. Repeat with the remaining rice and salmon.

Serve immediately with ponzu sauce for dipping.

sesame-coated chicken paillards and crispy salad

MAKES 4 SERVINGS

A paillard is the perfect way to cook chicken breasts. You have to do a little work on the front end—pounding—but then cooking them only takes about two minutes each. Plus, because they are so thin and in the hot sauté pan for such a short period of time, they stay tender and juicy. Here the sesame seeds give the paillards an extra-crunchy coating. You can serve these topped with any type of salad. I have called for crispy lettuce with fresh summer produce and a mildly acidic Meyer lemon dressing, but really use up whatever you have in the fridge—you can't go wrong! The paillards can be pounded up to one day in advance; store tightly wrapped in plastic wrap, in the refrigerator.

4 small boneless, skinless chicken breasts

½ cup toasted hulled white sesame seeds

Kosher salt and freshly ground black pepper

5 tablespoons olive oil, divided

4 heads little gem lettuce, leaves separated or 1 small head Bibb lettuce, leaves torn

1 pint cherry tomatoes, halved

1 Kirby cucumber, halved and sliced

3 tablespoons fresh Meyer lemon juice

Working one piece at a time, with the flat side of a meat mallet, pound the chicken between 2 pieces of plastic wrap or a zip-top bag cut open on 3 sides, to ⅛ to ¼ inch thick. Discard the plastic and sprinkle both sides of the paillards with the sesame seeds, pressing to help them adhere. Season with salt and pepper.

Heat a large sauté pan over high heat for 30 seconds. Add 1 tablespoon of the oil and heat for 10 seconds. Cook the paillards, in 4 batches, adding 1 teaspoon of oil to the sauté pan between each batch, until golden-brown on one side, 1 to 3 minutes. Turn and cook until cooked through, about 30 seconds (lower the heat if the pan becomes too dark).

Toss together the lettuce, tomatoes, cucumber, lemon juice, and the remaining 3 tablespoons of oil in a bowl. Season with salt and pepper.

Divide the paillards between four plates and top with the salad.

za'atar lamb chops with roasted beets and greens

MAKES 4 SERVINGS

A bunch of beets with the greens attached do double duty. Roast the beets and stems and sauté the greens (they taste, well, like beets and their texture is similar to Swiss chard). No greens attached? Use a small bunch of Swiss chard. Argan oil is best known as a beauty product, but food-grade bottles shouldn't be overlooked for their culinary applications. Its flavor is intensely nutty—similar to toasted sesame oil. That said, it may be difficult to locate, so feel free to substitute toasted sesame oil.

1 bunch beets with beet greens attached (see tips for prep instructions)

2 tablespoons olive oil, divided

Kosher salt and freshly ground black pepper

8 lamb chops (about 2½ pounds), 1 inch thick

2 teaspoons za'atar spice mix

1 tablespoon red wine vinegar

1 cup labneh

4 teaspoons toasted hulled white sesame seeds

Fresh mint leaves and argan or sesame oil, for garnish

Preheat oven to 425°F.

Toss the beetroots with 1 tablespoon of the oil. Season with salt and pepper. Roast on a rimmed baking sheet until just starting to soften, 14 to 16 minutes. Add the beet stems to the sheet and toss to coat with oil. Continue to roast until the beetroots and stems are tender, 14 to 16 minutes more.

While the beets roast, cook the lamb. Season the lamb with za'atar and salt and pepper. Heat a large sauté pan over high heat for 30 seconds. Add the remaining tablespoon of oil and heat for 10 seconds. Cook the lamb, in 2 batches, turning once, until medium rare, 6 to 10 minutes. Transfer to a plate to rest.

Add the beet greens to the sauté pan. Season with salt and pepper. Cook until just wilted, 1 to 2 minutes. Add the vinegar and toss to combine.

Serve the beetroots, stems, and greens with the lamb over the labneh. Sprinkle with the sesame seeds and garnish with mint and argan or sesame oil.

TIP *Peel the beetroots, then cut into ½-inch wedges. Remove the stems from the beet greens and cut into 2-inch lengths. Tear the greens into bite-sized pieces.*

TIP *For the most elegant presentation use frenched lamp chops. These chops have had all the meat, fat, or connective tissue attached to the bone removed.*

brussels sprouts carbonara with guanciale

Brussels sprouts can be a bit polarizing. I suspect that's because of the odorous, boiled-till-mush version from most folks' childhood. When roasted or quickly sautéed though, Brussels sprouts' best qualities (intense green flavor and snappy texture) are allowed to really shine through. Pair them with guanciale (an Italian cured meat product made from pork jowl or cheeks) and creamy egg yolks, and I guarantee that even lifelong Brussels sprouts haters will become converts. Don't forget to add a copious amount of freshly cracked black pepper to the finished dish; the "coal" acts as a balance to the rich eggs and cheese.

Kosher salt and freshly ground black pepper

2 ounces guanciale or pancetta, coarsely chopped

½ pound Brussels sprouts, leaves separated

2 tablespoons black sesame seeds

¾ pound short pasta

1 large egg plus 4 large egg yolks

2 ounces Parmesan, finely grated, plus more for serving

Bring a large pasta pot of salted water to a boil.

Cook the guanciale in a large straight-sided sauté pan over medium heat, stirring occasionally, until crispy, 10 to 12 minutes. Add the Brussels sprouts and sesame seeds to the sauté pan. Season with salt and pepper. Cook, stirring until bright green and crisp tender, 1 to 2 minutes.

One to two minutes after starting the guanciale, start cooking the pasta: Add the pasta to the boiling water and cook until al dente.

Remove the sauté pan from the heat. Use a spider or large slotted spoon to transfer the cooked pasta to the sauté pan. Add the egg and egg yolks, Parmesan, and enough pasta water to help create a sauce (between ¼ and ½ cup). Stir until the sauce coats the pasta and the cheese is melted. Season with salt and generously with pepper.

Serve topped with grated Parmesan.

TIP *Individual Brussels sprouts leaves look very pleasing in this pasta, but it can take a bit of time to separate them all. The quickest way to do it is to trim the root end, pull off as many leaves as you can, trim the root end again, repeat. If you're in a hurry, shred the Brussels sprouts, either with a knife or food processor.*

TIP *Since it can take 15 to 20 minutes for a large pot of water to come to a boil, I like to get the water boiling while I prep my ingredients. In this case, the pasta will take about the same amount of time to cook as the guanciale, so starting cooking the pasta 1 or 2 minutes after you start sautéing the guanciale.*

low-country-style sesame and honey baby back ribs

MAKES 4 SERVINGS

The flavoring on these ribs is tangy South Carolina style, with mustard and vinegar and a little something extra—sesame seeds. Slowly cooking the ribs in the oven, essentially braising them, ensures that they get super tender before going on the grill. No grill? Broil the ribs, basting occasionally with the sauce until glazed. The ribs can be braised up to two days in advance. Bring them to room temperature before grilling.

2 teaspoons sweet paprika

2 teaspoons dry mustard

1 teaspoon cayenne pepper

Kosher salt and freshly ground black pepper

2 racks baby back pork ribs (about 3 pounds)

½ cup Dijon mustard

⅓ cup apple cider vinegar

⅓ cup honey

¼ cup toasted hulled white sesame seeds

Preheat oven to 275°F. Combine the paprika, mustard, cayenne pepper, 3 teaspoons salt, and 1 teaspoon pepper in a bowl.

Rub both sides of the ribs with the spice rub. Transfer to a large, rimmed baking sheet or baking dish (it's OK if the racks overlap slightly) and cover tightly with foil. Bake until a fork easily slides into the meat, 2 to 2½ hours.

Combine the Dijon mustard, vinegar, honey, and sesame seeds in a bowl. Season with salt and pepper.

Heat grill to medium-high heat and set up for direct grilling (see page 9 for tips). Grill the ribs, basting both sides with the sauce and turning occasionally, until glazed and just beginning to char, 4 to 5 minutes.

> **TIP** *If your ribs still have the membrane attached, be sure to remove it before popping them in the oven. Simply loosen the membrane at one end of the rack with a knife. Grab the loosened membrane with a paper towel and peel it off the length of the rack.*

soba noodles with bok choy and sesame tempura shrimp

Though deep-fried these extra-crispy tempura shrimp have a very light texture. Pair with hearty buckwheat noodles, crunchy vegetables, and ponzu sauce for a refreshing lunch or dinner. The soba can be cooked one day ahead. It will stick together as it cools but simply run it under cold water to loosen.

2 heads baby bok choy, quartered through the root end

¾ pound soba noodles

5 cups canola oil

1 cup cake flour, spooned and leveled

¼ cup toasted hulled white sesame seeds, plus more for serving

1 teaspoon baking powder

¼ teaspoon baking soda

1 cup all-purpose flour, spooned and leveled, divided

2 cups cold seltzer water

Kosher salt

12 jumbo shrimp (about ½ pound), peeled, leaving the tail shell attached, and deveined

½ cup shredded daikon radish

2 scallions, sliced

Sliced red chile or sambal, for serving

Ponzu (page 205)

Set a steamer basket in a large stockpot. Fill the pot with 2 inches of water and bring to a simmer. Add the bok choy and steam until tender, 4 to 6 minutes. Transfer to a plate and cool to room temperature.

Cook the soba according to the directions on the package. Drain and rinse under cold water to prevent the noodles from sticking together.

Heat the oil in a small saucepan to 375°F (the oil should be about 1½ inches deep).

While the oil is heating, make the tempura batter. Whisk together the cake flour, sesame seeds, baking powder, baking soda, and ½ cup of the all-purpose flour in a bowl. Add the seltzer and stir until just combined (the batter will be thin and a little lumpy). Place the remaining ½ cup of all-purpose flour in a shallow bowl.

Season the shrimp with salt. Working with one shrimp at a time, grab a shrimp by the tail and dip it in the flour and then in the batter. Fry, up to 4 shrimp at a time, until golden-brown, 2 to 4 minutes. Drain on paper towels.

Serve the noodles topped with the bok choy, shrimp, daikon, scallions, chile, and sesame seeds, drizzled with the ponzu sauce.

TIP *It's important that the seltzer water is ice cold when making the tempura batter. This prevents the gluten in the flour from forming, which ensures a light batter and crust. It's also prudent not to overmix the batter; it should be lumpy and thin.*

TIP *If you don't have an oil thermometer, you can dip the tip of an instant-read thermometer in the oil to test the temperature.*

SESAME

buttery sesame cookies

MAKES 30 COOKIES

These extra-buttery, crispy-on-the-outside, soft-in-the-middle wonderfully addictive cookies are similar to the classic benne wafer, only larger. Serve them with tea or creamy coffee, or try them as sandwiches with a little of your favorite ice cream as filler (the Black Sesame Seed and Ginger Ice Cream, page 36, is a natural choice) for a yummy summer treat. Store in an airtight container, at room temperature, for three days.

1 cup all-purpose flour, spooned and leveled

¼ teaspoon baking soda

½ teaspoon kosher salt

10 tablespoons unsalted butter, at room temperature

¾ cup packed light-brown sugar

¼ cup granulated sugar

1 large egg, at room temperature

½ teaspoon pure vanilla extract

1 cup toasted hulled white sesame seeds

Preheat oven to 350°F. Line 2 rimmed baking sheets with parchment. Whisk together the flour, baking soda, and salt in a bowl.

Beat the butter and sugars with an electric mixer on medium-high speed until light and fluffy, 2 to 3 minutes. Add the egg and beat until fully incorporated. Add the vanilla and beat to combine. Reduce the mixer speed to low and gradually beat in the flour mixture. Add the sesame seeds and beat to combine.

Drop tablespoons of the dough, 3 inches apart, on the lined baking sheet. Bake, rotating the sheets front to back and top to bottom halfway through, until golden-brown, 5 to 6 minutes.

Cool the cookies on the baking sheet for 5 minutes then transfer to a cooling rack to cool completely.

black sesame seed and ginger ice cream

MAKES 3 CUPS

Homemade ice cream is a thing of wonder. It's not only creamy and fresh (no freezer burn, please!), it gives you the freedom to create any flavor combination you can dream up. The unusual flavors—spicy and nutty—in this recipe make it the perfect choice for the chilled dessert adventurous. The moisture in the agave helps the poppy seeds grind down into a smooth paste, while the granulated sugar provides the right amount of sweetness. Chill the ice-cream base by popping it in the fridge or quick chill it by placing it in a bowl over an ice bath and stirring often. The base can be made up to two days in advance; store in an airtight container, in the refrigerator.

⅓ cup black sesame seeds

2 tablespoons agave

2 cups heavy cream

1 cup whole milk

¾ cup sugar

¼ cup sliced fresh ginger

Pinch kosher salt

6 large egg yolks

Place the sesame seeds in a food processor. Process until broken down, 3 to 5 minutes. Add the agave and process until a smooth paste forms, 2 to 3 minutes (you should have ¼ cup of paste). Set aside.

Combine the cream, milk, sugar, ginger, and salt in a medium saucepan. Simmer, stirring occasionally, until the sugar is melted, 2 to 3 minutes. Remove from heat and let steep 15 minutes. Strain through a fine mesh sieve (discard ginger) and return to the pot.

Set a clean fine mesh sieve over a bowl. Whisk together the eggs in a separate bowl.

Return the cream mixture to a simmer. Slowly whisk 1 cup of the cream mixture into the eggs to temper them. Return the tempered egg mixture to the remaining cream mixture and whisk to combine. Cook over medium-low heat, stirring constantly, until thickened (a line drawn through the custard on the back of a spoon should not fill back in), 10 to 12 minutes. Remove from the heat and strain through the prepared sieve.

Whisk 1 cup of the custard into the black sesame paste. Return to the remaining custard and whisk to combine. Chill completely.

Turn the ice cream according to the directions for your ice-cream machine.

Transfer to an airtight container and freeze until firm, at least 3 hours.

TIP *Be sure to cook the custard over a low flame to avoid curdling it. Tempering is the process of slowly whisking a little of a warm liquid into uncooked, whisked eggs before returning it to the larger batch of warm liquid. This technique gently warms the eggs and prevents them from scrambling.*

SESAME

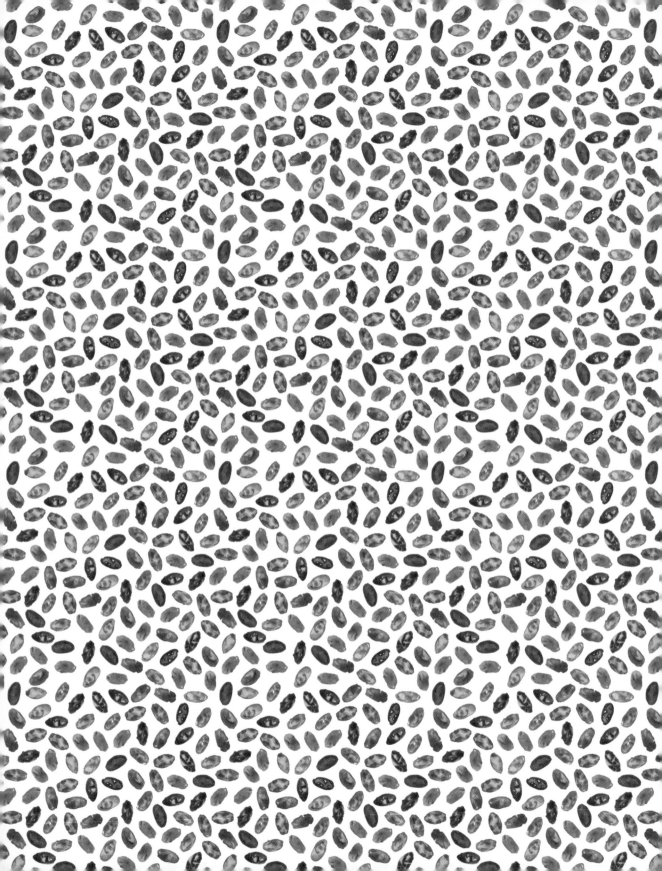

CHIA

The tiny yet mighty chia has been around the block! Yes, it is the same little seed that creates a magical, hair-like rug covering your Chia Pet, but chia seeds have actually been around for millennia. A staple of the Aztec and Mayan diets in pre-Columbian times, chia seeds were found in the survival ration pouches on the belts of Aztec warriors, who would eat small quantities of them throughout the day for their high energy and protein content. Modern-day athletes, like the legendary Tarahumara runners, rely on a chia drink for strength and stamina. Grown in central Mexico for centuries, not only was chia a highly coveted food source, it was also used for medicinal purposes and even as currency.

Chia is incredibly high in heart-healthy omega-3 and omega-6 fatty acids. It's also rich in protein, vitamin B complex, especially niacin (vitamin B3) and riboflavin (vitamin B2), calcium, potassium, and fiber. The oil pressed from chia seeds is incredibly nutrient dense; 60 percent is made up of omega-3 fatty acids. The oil has a neutral flavor, which makes it a perfect choice as a substitute for canola oil in Asian dressing. Because it can be quite expensive, I typically replace only a small quantity of canola or olive oil in a recipe with chia oil.

When mixed with liquid, chia forms a gel-like substance. Amazingly, this same reaction occurs in the stomach when the seeds are consumed. This helps to slow the breakdown of carbohydrates into sugar, which allows you to feel fuller longer and prevent overeating. While developing the recipes for this chapter, I found the gel-forming property of chia beneficial in the right circumstances—for example, the Peanut and Double Chocolate Chia Pudding (page 59)

and the Cucumber and Basil Chia Fresca (page 59). But in other applications, too much chia is not a good thing. A few tablespoons nicely thickens and adds body to the sauce in the Harissa-Braised Chicken Legs (page 57), but more would cause the sauce to become gloppy. That said, given that even a small quantity of chia provides tons of nutritional benefits, a dash here and a sprinkle there will make breakfast, a snack, or dinner even more delicious and nutritious.

TASTE, TEXTURE, APPEARANCE

Though chia is related to both mint and sage, it lacks any distinctive herbal flavor. The taste is mild and just the tiniest bit nutty. The diminutive seeds are mostly dark brown and black, though there are always a handful of lighter colored ones floating around in each bag. Their texture is über crunchy, which lends an extra layer of delicious crispiness to the Chia-Crusted Eggplant Parm Stacks (page 51) and Two-Seed Oatmeal Chocolate-Chip Cookies (page 60).

BUYING AND KEEPING

Chia seeds are available packaged in most grocery stores, in bulk at health-food stores, and also online. Like all foods rich in antioxidants, the oil in chia seeds is very slow to oxidize, thus the seeds can be stored for years without deteriorating. Store chia in an airtight container, at room temperature in a dark and cool place, for two years. Once the oil has been separated from the seed, though, it becomes quite unstable, thus it should not be heated. Instead, try it in vinaigrettes or smoothies. Store the oil in a cool, dark place for six months.

TOASTING INSTRUCTIONS

Toasting chia seeds will make their flavor slightly more pronounced but may hinder their gel-forming qualities. Toast the seeds in a medium sauté pan over low heat, stirring, until slightly fragrant, two to three minutes. For best results, toast seeds just before using.

chia milk

MAKES 2½ CUPS

When you add liquid to chia, it thickens and becomes gel-like. A thick milk might not be to everyone's liking, so I balanced the amount of chia here to make it less dense. (If you do like a thicker milk, add up to one-third cup chia seeds). Use this milk anywhere you would use cow's milk; I like it in my morning coffee or with a bit of muesli. As with all seed milk recipes, you can adjust the salt and sweetener to your liking. Store in an airtight container, in the refrigerator, for one week.

¼ cup toasted chia seeds
1 tablespoon agave
Kosher salt

Place the chia seeds and 3 cups of water in a bowl. Soak overnight in the refrigerator; drain.

Place the soaked chia seeds, agave, a pinch of salt, and 3 cups of water in a blender. Blend on high until very smooth, 2 to 3 minutes.

Strain the milk through a nut milk bag or a very fine mesh metal strainer. Chill completely.

minty chia pear smoothie

Tangy and bright, the combination of mint and pear make for a flavorful morning drink or afternoon pick-me-up. Be sure to use a ripe, or even an overripe, pear. And don't peel it; there is a lot of fiber in the skin. Drink it right away or it will get too thick!

1 pear, cored and chopped

1 cup pear juice

⅓ cup fresh mint leaves

2 tablespoons toasted chia

Place the pear, pear juice, mint, chia, and ½-cup of ice cubes in a blender. Blend on high until very smooth, 30 seconds.

chia pecan butter

While this nut butter won't win any beauty contests—the chia seeds give it a speckled appearance—it might win a blue ribbon for taste. Try it on apple slices with a little drizzle of honey or spread on waffles and topped with a sprinkle of berries. Pecans are soft, so it takes less time to process this butter than others in the book. Store in an airtight container, in the refrigerator, for two months.

2 cups raw pecans

½ cup toasted chia seeds, finely ground in a spice grinder

Kosher salt

Preheat oven to 350°F. Spread the pecans on a small, rimmed baking sheet. Toast, until just beginning to smell fragrant, 8 to 10 minutes. Cool to room temperature.

Place the cooled pecans and chia seeds in a food processor. Process, stopping the food processor and scraping down the bowl as necessary, until the butter is smooth and creamy, about 4 to 6 minutes. Season with salt.

arugula, walnut, and chia pesto

MAKES 1¼ CUPS

Arugula gives this pesto a hint of spice, and the oily walnuts make it rich and creamy. If you don't have both Pecorino and Parmesan (or don't feel like buying both), you can use all Parm, though the flavor will not be as complex. Try it over seared salmon or, of course, tossed in pasta; it's also an excellent topping for flatbread (see Whole Wheat Flatbread with Chia Pesto, Ricotta Salata, and Radishes, page 54). Store in an airtight container, in the refrigerator, for one week. If the pesto thickens too much during storage, thin by stirring in a tablespoon of oil or water.

¼ cup raw walnuts

2 packed cups baby arugula

1 tablespoon toasted chia seeds

1 ounce Parmesan, grated

1 ounce Pecorino, grated

1 garlic clove

½ cup olive oil

Kosher salt and freshly ground black pepper

Preheat oven to 350°F. Spread the walnuts on a small, rimmed baking sheet. Toast, until just beginning to smell fragrant, 8 to 10 minutes.

Place the walnuts, arugula, chia seeds, Parmesan, Pecorino, garlic, and ¼ cup of water in a blender. Blend on medium high, stopping the blender and scraping down the jar as necessary, until the mixture is almost smooth, 30 seconds to 1 minute. With the blender running, slowly add the oil through the feed tube. Process until the pesto is smooth, 10 to 20 seconds. Season with salt and pepper.

chia, fennel seed, and thyme shake

MAKES ¼ CUP

This shake has a bright licorice flavor from the fennel and savory notes from the chia and thyme. Try it on hearty winter soups and stews, sprinkled on pizza dough before topping and baking, or tossed on roasted vegetables. I use it in my recipe for Chia-Crusted Eggplant Parm Stacks (page 51). Store in an airtight container, at room temperature, for two months.

2 tablespoons toasted chia seeds, coarsely ground in a spice grinder

1 tablespoon fennel seeds, crushed or coarsely ground in a spice grinder

1 teaspoon dried thyme

Kosher salt and freshly ground black pepper

Combine the chia seeds, fennel, and thyme in a bowl. Season with salt and pepper.

tomato tamarind dip

MAKES 2 CUPS

If you haven't cooked with tamarind before, give it a shot: It's just a little sweet but also has a slight sour note—think of a combination of a lemon and a date. The spices in the dip nod toward Indian food, making it a perfect accompaniment for curries or roasted vegetables and rice. That said, it's also great served with pita chips or crackers for dipping. Store in an airtight container, in the refrigerator, for two days.

Kosher salt

1¾ pounds tomatoes

3 tablespoons olive oil

1 small yellow onion, chopped

2 garlic cloves, chopped

1 teaspoon finely grated fresh ginger

½ teaspoon red pepper flakes

¼ teaspoon mustard seeds

2 tablespoons tamarind paste or chopped, seedless tamarind pulp

1 tablespoon toasted chia seeds

TIP *When working with tamarind, even if the package says seedless, be sure it really is before you start chopping: I have found the occasional stray seed, and if you hit one with your knife, it can take a chunk out of the blade. Store leftover tamarind at room temperature for up to one year.*

Bring a medium saucepan of salted water to a boil. Set a bowl of ice water nearby.

Core the tomatoes and cut a small, shallow X in the root end. Boil the tomatoes until the skin loosens, 15 to 20 seconds. Use a spider or slotted spoon to transfer to the ice water. Once the tomatoes are cool, peel away the skin; discard. Halve the tomatoes and squeeze out the seeds; discard the seeds. Chop the flesh.

Heat a large sauté pan over medium heat for 30 seconds. Add the oil and heat for 10 seconds. Add the onion. Season with salt. Cook, stirring occasionally, until tender, 10 to 12 minutes. Add the garlic and ginger. Cook, stirring, until fragrant, 30 seconds. Add the pepper flakes and mustard seeds. Cook, stirring, 30 seconds. Add the chopped tomatoes, tamarind, and chia seeds. Increase the heat to medium-high and cook, stirring occasionally, until the tomatoes have broken down and thickened, 9 to 11 minutes.

Transfer the mixture to a food processor. Process until the tomatoes are smooth, 10 to 15 seconds. Season with salt.

Serve at room temperature.

low-sugar fig and chia jam

MAKES 1½ CUPS

This is a lightly sweet and savory jam; the rosemary gives it a warm, herbaceous flavor, while the lemon zest adds a bright, floral note. Try it on toast with ricotta for breakfast, or put a small bowl alongside a cheese plate. If your figs are not quite ripe, you can help them break down faster by mashing them with a potato masher during cooking. Use any type of fresh figs, but I think Missions make the prettiest jam. Store in an airtight container, in the refrigerator, for two weeks.

1 pound ripe fresh figs, stems discarded and chopped

2 tablespoons honey

1 tablespoon chia seeds

1 sprig fresh rosemary

1 strip lemon zest and 2 teaspoons lemon juice

⅛ teaspoon kosher salt

Combine the figs, honey, chia seeds, rosemary, lemon zest and juice, and salt in a small saucepan. Cook over medium heat until the figs start to break down, 10 to 12 minutes. Discard the rosemary and lemon zest.

Chill completely.

blueberry chia muffins

These muffins are chock-full of tasty goodness—pecans, coconut, oats, gobs of blueberries, and, of course, protein-rich chia. They have bumpy, rough-looking tops, but the insides are super moist. I like to sweeten with grade B maple syrup; it's not only cheaper, but it has more flavor and minerals than grade A (but if grade A syrup is what you have, don't sweat it). Store in an airtight container, at room temperature, for three days.

½ cup unsweetened flaked coconut

½ cup pecans, roughly chopped

1¼ cups white whole wheat flour, spooned and leveled

1 cup old-fashioned rolled oats

¼ cup chia seeds

1 teaspoon ground cinnamon

1 teaspoon baking powder

1 teaspoon baking soda

1 teaspoon kosher salt

1 cup sour cream

½ cup pure grade B maple syrup

6 tablespoons unsalted butter, melted

1 large egg

1 teaspoon pure vanilla extract

1 pint blueberries

Preheat oven to 350°F. Line a 12-cup standard muffin tin with liners.

Spread the coconut on a small, rimmed baking sheet. Spread the pecans on a separate rimmed baking sheet. Toast, tossing once until the coconut is brown and the pecans are fragrant, 6 to 8 minutes for the coconut and 8 to 10 minutes for the pecans. Cool to room temperature.

Whisk together the flour, oats, chia, cinnamon, baking powder, baking soda, and salt in a bowl. Whisk together the sour cream, maple syrup, butter, egg, and vanilla in a separate bowl. Add the wet ingredients to the dry ingredients and stir to combine. Fold in the blueberries, coconut, and pecans.

Divide the batter between the lined cups (about ⅓ cup each). Bake, rotating the tins halfway, until a toothpick inserted in the center comes out clean, 24 to 26 minutes.

Set the tin on a wire rack and let the muffins cool in the pan for 5 minutes. After 5 minutes, transfer the muffins to the wire rack.

Eat warm or at room temperature.

toasted sorghum with shiitakes and fried eggs

MAKES 4 SERVINGS

Fried eggs make this a wonderful breakfast or brunch dish—but it's a delicious lunch or dinner, too. Sorghum—an ancient, gluten-free cereal grain with small, round seeds—maintains a slightly chewy texture when cooked. I highly recommend searching it out, but if you can't find it in your local health-food market, use one cup of brown rice instead. Stirring the chia seeds in at the end, rather than cooking them in from the beginning, ensures that the mixture doesn't become gummy.

3 tablespoons canola oil, divided

2 scallions, white and green parts separated, sliced

Kosher salt and freshly ground black pepper

½ cup long-grain brown rice

½ cup sorghum

2 cups chicken stock (page 203)

2 tablespoons toasted chia seeds

7 ounces shiitake mushrooms, stems discarded and sliced

2 garlic cloves, chopped

1 tablespoon unseasoned rice vinegar

1 teaspoon soy sauce, plus more for serving

4 large eggs

1 avocado, sliced

Sriracha and lime wedges, for serving

Heat a small saucepan over medium heat for 30 seconds. Add 1 tablespoon of the oil and heat for 10 seconds. Add the scallion whites. Season with salt and pepper. Cook, stirring occasionally, until tender, 1 to 2 minutes. Add the brown rice and sorghum. Cook, stirring occasionally, until toasted and fragrant, 3 to 4 minutes. Add the stock and bring to a boil. Cover the saucepan, reduce the heat to low, and gently simmer until the grains are tender, 50 to 55 minutes. Remove from the heat. Sprinkle the chia seeds on top of the grains. Cover and let stand for 10 minutes. Fluff with a fork, incorporating the seeds into the grains.

Once you have sprinkled the chia seeds on the grains, heat 1 tablespoon of oil in a large nonstick sauté pan over medium-high heat. Add the shiitakes and garlic. Cook, stirring occasionally, until the mushrooms are golden-brown, 5 to 7 minutes. Stir in the vinegar and soy sauce. Season with salt and pepper. Transfer to a plate; reserve the skillet.

Heat the remaining tablespoon of oil over medium heat in the reserved skillet. Crack the eggs in the skillet, being sure to space them apart. Season with salt and pepper. Cook, covered, until the whites are set but the yolks are still runny, 2 to 4 minutes.

Serve the mushrooms and eggs over the grains, drizzled with a squeeze of Sriracha, and garnished with the scallion greens, avocado, and lime wedges.

mango chia pancakes

MAKES 4 SERVINGS

These golden, fruit-speckled pancakes are incredibly moist and tender because of the gel that forms between the mango and chia. If you love the flavor of maple but don't want to use syrup, serve up a stack sprinkled with the Maple Flax Pecan Shake.

¾ cup white whole wheat flour, spooned and leveled

½ cup all-purpose flour, spooned and leveled

2 tablespoons toasted chia seeds

2 teaspoons baking powder

2 tablespoons granulated sugar

½ teaspoon kosher salt

1 cup buttermilk

2 tablespoons unsalted butter, melted, plus more for the pan and for serving

1 large egg

1 cup finely chopped mango (from 1 mango, peeled and pitted)

Maple Flax Pecan Shake (page 69), for serving (optional)

Preheat oven to 200°F and place a baking sheet inside.

Whisk together the flours, chia seeds, baking powder, sugar, and salt in a bowl. Whisk together the buttermilk, butter, and egg in a bowl. Add the wet ingredients to the dry ingredients and whisk to combine. Stir in the mango.

Heat a large nonstick sauté pan over medium heat until hot. Dip a pastry brush or balled-up paper towel in butter and lightly grease the bottom of the pan.

Using ¼ cup of batter for each pancake, spoon into the sauté pan and smooth to make round (you should be able to fit 4 pancakes in the pan). Cook until golden-brown, 6 to 8 minutes. Flip and cook until cooked through, 6 to 8 minutes. Transfer to the baking sheet. Repeat with the remaining batter, buttering the pan between each batch.

Serve topped with butter and the maple syrup shake, if desired.

> **TIP** *Be sure to use a mango that is just ripe—it should be soft without any brown spots or bruises. Since the mangoes in the grocery store are often as hard as hockey pucks, you'll want to plan ahead. For Saturday morning pancakes, buy your underripe mango two to three days ahead. Wrap it in a small paper bag (the bag traps the ethylene the fruit gives off, which helps it ripen faster): come Saturday morning, voilà!*

chia-crusted eggplant parm stacks

MAKES 4 SERVINGS

Baked versions of dishes that are normally fried (for example, eggplant and chicken parmesan) are typically not as crunchy nor nearly as delicious. I guarantee that's not the case here. The chia makes the crust in these eggplant stacks extra crispy, and the buttery tomato sauce makes it over-the-top decadent. If you want to take it to the next level, top half of the finished eggplant slices with a small piece of mozzarella and bake until just melted, about four minutes. Serve as a starter or make it dinner by serving with a fresh green salad. The sauce can be made and the eggplant slices can be baked (but not coated) two days ahead; store in an airtight container, in the refrigerator.

2 tablespoons unsalted butter

2 garlic cloves, chopped

1 28-ounce can whole peeled tomatoes

1 sprig fresh basil, plus small leaves for serving

1 cup panko breadcrumbs

3 tablespoons olive oil, divided

Kosher salt and freshly ground black pepper

1 ounce Parmesan, grated, plus 1 1-inch piece rind

2 tablespoons chia seeds

2 small to medium eggplants (¾ pound), sliced

⅓ cup all-purpose flour

2 large eggs, beaten

Chia, Fennel Seed, and Thyme Shake (page 43), for serving

Preheat oven to 450°F.

Melt the butter in a medium saucepan over medium heat. Add the garlic and cook until fragrant, 30 seconds. Add the tomatoes, basil, and Parmesan rind. Season with salt and pepper. Break the tomatoes into small pieces with a potato masher. Bring to a boil. Reduce the heat and simmer, stirring occasionally, until thickened slightly, 14 to 16 minutes. Keep warm.

While the sauce is simmering, make the eggplant: Toss the panko with 1 tablespoon of the oil. Season with salt and pepper. Toast, tossing once, until golden-brown, 2 to 4 minutes. Transfer to a shallow bowl and cool to room temperature. Add the chia seeds and grated Parmesan and toss to combine.

Toss the eggplant with the remaining 2 tablespoons of oil. Season with salt and pepper. Bake on a rimmed baking sheet, turning once, until almost tender, 10 to 12 minutes.

Line a rimmed baking sheet with an oven-proof cooling rack.

Place the flour on a plate and the eggs in a shallow bowl. Working one piece at a time, coat the eggplant in the flour, dip in the egg (allowing any excess to drip off), and coat in the panko mixture. Place on the cooling rack. Repeat with the remaining eggplant.

Bake until the eggplant is tender, 10 to 12 minutes.

Serve the eggplant over the sauce, topped with basil leaves and the shake.

caesar salad with egg-free dressing

MAKES 4 SERVINGS

Classic Caesar dressing is usually made directly in a wooden salad bowl in which the lettuce leaves and other ingredients are tossed. In this case, we make the dressing in a blender so that the oil can be slowly added through the feed tube—ensuring a beautifully emulsified dressing. Don't make this dressing ahead; it gets too thick and gloppy.

½ loaf sourdough bread (4 ounces), torn into ¾-inch pieces

½ teaspoon cayenne pepper

½ cup plus 3 tablespoons olive oil, divided

Kosher salt and freshly ground black pepper

4 anchovy fillets

2 garlic cloves, chopped

1 tablespoon fresh lemon juice

1 teaspoon Worcestershire sauce

1 tablespoon chia seeds, finely ground in a spice grinder

½ teaspoon Dijon mustard

1 head romaine lettuce, torn

2 ounces Parmesan, grated

Preheat oven to 400°F.

Toss together the bread, cayenne pepper, and 2 tablespoons of the oil. Season with salt and black pepper. Toast on a rimmed baking sheet, tossing once, until golden-brown and crispy, 10 to 12 minutes. Cool to room temperature.

While the croutons are cooking, make the dressing: Place the anchovies, garlic, lemon juice, Worcestershire, chia seeds, Dijon, and 1 tablespoon of the oil in a blender. Process until combined. With the blender running, slowly add the remaining ½ cup of oil through the feed tube. Season with salt and black pepper.

Toss together the dressing, croutons, romaine, and Parmesan. Season with salt and pepper.

whole wheat flatbread with chia pesto, ricotta salata, and radishes

Think of a flatbread as a blank canvas: You can use any type of paint you want (tomato sauce, pesto) and throw on all kinds of three-dimensional objects (cheese, greens, cooked sausage, and even nuts). The combo I use in this recipe has a nice balance of salty, creamy, crunchy, and spicy, but truly, you can top it with anything you like. If you don't have a grill, or want to make this inside during the winter months, use a grill pan heated over medium-high heat.

½ recipe pizza dough (page 202)

2 tablespoons toasted chia seeds

⅓ cup olive oil

2 dried chiles de arbol

2 garlic cloves, smashed

2 sprigs fresh rosemary

Kosher salt

All-purpose flour, for the work surface

½ cup Arugula, Walnut, and Chia Pesto (page 43)

4 ounces ricotta salata, shaved with a vegetable peeler

⅓ cup oil-cured olives, halved

¼ cup toasted pine nuts

2 radishes, thinly sliced

Make the pizza dough, substituting the white whole wheat flour with whole wheat flour and adding the chia seeds with the flour mixture.

Combine the oil, chiles, garlic, and rosemary in a small saucepan. Cook over medium heat until the garlic and rosemary are sizzling, 1 to 3 minutes. Season with salt.

Heat grill to medium-high heat.

Divide the dough into four pieces. On a floured work surface, press or roll the dough into 8-inch circles.

Place as many pieces of dough as will fit directly over the heat. Brush with some of the garlic chile oil. Grill until puffed and golden-brown and crispy of the bottom, 1 to 3 minutes. Flip and brush the cooked side with some of the garlic chile oil. Grill until the dough is cooked through, 1 to 3 minutes. Repeat with the remaining dough and oil.

Top the flatbreads with the pesto, ricotta salata, olives, pine nuts, and radishes. Season with salt. Drizzle with any remaining oil.

harissa braised chicken legs

Store-bought harissas often don't have the same level of acidity that my homemade version does, so if you forgo making your own, be sure to stir the vinegar in at the end. It will give the dish a brightness and help balance the heat. My favorite way to eat this dish is to mash up the potatoes in the bottom of the bowl; this way I can soak up all the delicious, spicy sauce. Make this dish up to one day ahead. Store in an airtight container, in the refrigerator. Stir in chicken stock or water to thin, if necessary.

1 tablespoon olive oil

4 whole chicken legs (about 2½ pounds)

Kosher salt and freshly ground black pepper

1 onion, sliced

⅓ cup harissa (page 206)

1 cup chicken stock (page 203)

1½ pounds small Yukon gold potatoes, cut into 1¼-inch pieces

1 red bell pepper, sliced

1 sprig fresh oregano, plus leaves for serving

2 tablespoons toasted chia seeds

1 bay leaf

1 tablespoon red wine vinegar, optional

Heat a large Dutch oven over medium-high heat for 30 seconds. Add the oil and heat for 10 seconds. Season the chicken with salt and pepper. Brown, skin-side down, in 2 batches, until golden-brown, 14 to 16 minutes. Transfer to a plate.

Add the onion to the Dutch oven. Season with salt and pepper. Cook, scraping up any brown bits stuck on the bottom of the pan and stirring occasionally, until tender, 4 to 5 minutes. Add the *harissa*. Cook, stirring occasionally, until slightly thickened, 3 to 5 minutes.

Add the stock, potatoes, bell pepper, oregano, chia seeds, and bay leaf. Top with the chicken, skin-side up. Bring to a boil. Reduce the heat and simmer, partially covered, until the potatoes are tender and the chicken is cooked through, 40 to 45 minutes. Discard the bay leaf and oregano. Stir in the vinegar, if desired.

Serve topped with oregano leaves.

> TIP *Instead of whole legs, you can use 8 bone-in, skin-on chicken thighs; brown in 2 batches as instructed.*

smoky bean chili

Chili isn't just for cold weather months. Try this protein-rich version (it's packed full of beans, quinoa, and chia) during the summer topped with tons of chopped tomatoes and cilantro and substitute the spinach for kale. The chia helps thicken it, giving it a rich mouthfeel, while stirring in greens at the end keeps the flavor fresh. Make this dish up to three days ahead (the flavors will really blend and meld); store in an airtight container, in the refrigerator. Stir in vegetable stock or water to thin, if necessary.

3 tablespoons olive oil

1 onion, chopped

2 garlic cloves, chopped

Kosher salt and freshly ground black pepper

2 poblano chiles, chopped

1 14.5-ounce can diced fire-roasted tomatoes, drained

2 tablespoons chili powder

2 teaspoons cumin seeds, finely ground in a spice grinder

3 cups vegetable stock (page 204)

2 14.5-ounce cans pink beans, drained and rinsed

¼ cup quinoa, rinsed

2 tablespoons chia seeds

3 cups torn kale leaves

Fresh cilantro leaves and tender stems, sour cream, Cheddar cheese, and whole grain tortilla chips, for serving

Heat a large saucepan over medium-high heat for 30 seconds. Add the oil and heat for 10 seconds. Add the onion and garlic. Season with salt and pepper. Cook, stirring occasionally, until soft, 9 to 10 minutes. Add the poblanos, tomatoes, chili powder, and cumin. Season with salt and pepper. Cook, stirring occasionally, until the poblanos are tender and the tomatoes are thickened, 6 to 8 minutes.

Add the stock, beans, quinoa, and chia seeds. Bring to a boil. Reduce the heat and simmer, stirring occasionally, until the quinoa is tender and the liquid is thickened, 24 to 26 minutes. Stir in the kale.

Top with the cilantro, sour cream, and Cheddar cheese. Serve with the chips.

> **TIP** *Before using quinoa, be sure to give it a good, long rinse under cold water. This will rinse away some of that bitter taste that sometimes gives quinoa a bad rap.*

peanut and double chocolate chia pudding

MAKES 4 SERVINGS

This luscious dairy-free pudding is really easy to make. Even though it has to sit for a while to thicken and become pudding-like, not having to turn on the heat to cook it makes that extra time worth it. Unlike typical chocolate chia puddings, the chia seeds are blended here to give the pudding a smoother texture. Melted chocolate makes it extra rich and chocolatey. If you can't find Dutch-processed cocoa powder, substitute the natural variety. The pudding will have a lighter color, but will still be delicious.

1½ cups almond milk

¼ cup chia seeds

3 tablespoons agave

2 tablespoons Peanut Flax Butter (page 67)

2 tablespoons Dutch-processed cocoa powder

1 teaspoon pure vanilla extract

Pinch kosher salt

½ cup semisweet chocolate chips, melted

Shaved chocolate, for serving

Place the almond milk, chia seeds, agave, peanut flax butter, cocoa powder, vanilla, and salt in a blender. Blend on high until the chia seeds are ground, 30 seconds. With the machine running, slowly add the chocolate through the food tube. Process until combined, 10 to 15 seconds.

Transfer the pudding to a bowl. Cover and refrigerate until thickened, at least 6 hours and up to 3 days.

Serve topped with shaved chocolate.

cucumber and basil chia fresca

MAKES 2 SERVINGS

This summertime favorite has a beautiful deep-green color from the unpeeled cucumber and basil and tangy, refreshing flavor. Serve it with a splash of soda over ice to make it even more fresca. If your blender is not so powerful, give the cucumber a good chop before blending; this will prevent the blades from getting stuck.

1 English cucumber, chopped

1 packed cup fresh basil leaves

¼ cup agave

2 tablespoons fresh lemon juice

1 tablespoon chia seeds

Place the cucumber, basil, agave, lemon juice, and ¼ cup of water in a blender. Blend on high until very smooth, 30 seconds. Strain through a fine mesh sieve. Stir in the chia seeds. Refrigerate until chilled and the chia seeds have puffed slightly, at least 3 hours and up to 1 day.

two-seed oatmeal chocolate-chip cookies

MAKES 12 COOKIES

These large (about five inches) and seedy cookies have what I consider the perfect cookie texture—crunchy on the edges and soft in the middle. The sunflower seeds give them an extra-deep flavor and the chia seeds a bit of crunch throughout. The dough can be made, formed into balls, and frozen, up to two weeks ahead. Bake the frozen balls at 325°F for 14 to 16 minutes. Store baked cookies in an airtight container, at room temperature, for three days.

½ cup white whole wheat flour, spooned and leveled

½ cup all-purpose flour, spooned and leveled

¾ teaspoon kosher salt

½ teaspoon baking powder

¼ teaspoon baking soda

½ cup (1 stick) unsalted butter, at room temperature

½ cup packed light-brown sugar

¼ cup granulated sugar

1 large egg

1 teaspoon pure vanilla extract

½ cup old-fashioned rolled oats

¼ cup toasted sunflower seeds

2 tablespoons toasted chia seeds

1 cup semisweet chocolate chips

½ cup bittersweet chocolate chips

Preheat oven to 350°F. Line 2 rimmed baking sheets with parchment. Whisk together the flours, salt, baking powder, and baking soda in a bowl.

Beat the butter and sugars with an electric mixer on medium-high speed until light and fluffy, 2 to 3 minutes. Add the egg and beat until fully incorporated. Add the vanilla and beat to combine. Reduce the mixer speed to low and gradually beat in the flour mixture. Stir in the oats, sunflower seeds, chia seeds, and chocolate chips.

Drop ¼-cup mounds of the dough, 3 inches apart, on the lined baking sheet. Bake, rotating the sheets front to back and top to bottom halfway through, until golden-brown, 10 to 12 minutes.

Cool the cookies on the sheet trays for 5 minutes then transfer to a cooling rack to cool completely.

> **TIP** *If you want to increase the yield to 24, make each cookie smaller by using 2 tablespoons instead of ¼ cup. Reduce the cooking time by about 4 minutes.*

cherry almond blondies

MAKES 16 BARS

Blondies are like a cross between a pound cake and a brownie—rich, buttery, and dense. These have a great mix of savory flavor from the chia seeds and almonds and mild sweetness from the cherries. When prepping the cherries, be sure to shake out as much liquid as possible. This will help keep the blondies from getting soggy. Store in an airtight container, at room temperature, for up to three days.

1 cup (2 sticks) unsalted butter, at room temperature, plus more for the pan

1½ cups all-purpose flour, spooned and leveled

1 cup white whole wheat flour, spooned and leveled

2 tablespoons toasted chia seeds

1 teaspoon baking powder

½ teaspoon kosher salt

1½ cups packed light-brown sugar

2 large eggs

1 teaspoon pure vanilla extract

1 10-ounce bag frozen sweet cherries, defrosted, drained well, and coarsely chopped

½ cup roasted almonds, chopped

Preheat oven to 350°F.

Butter an 8-inch-square baking dish. Line with parchment, leaving an overhang on 2 sides to help lift the blondies from the pan. Butter the paper. Whisk together the flours, chia seeds, baking powder, and salt in a bowl.

Beat the butter and sugar with an electric mixer on medium-high speed until light and fluffy, 2 to 3 minutes. Add the eggs, one at a time, beating well between each addition to fully incorporate. Add the vanilla and beat to combine. Reduce the mixer speed to low and gradually beat in the flour mixture. Stir in the cherries and almonds.

Transfer the batter to the lined pan. Bake until a toothpick inserted in the center comes out clean, 45 to 50 minutes.

Cool the blondies in the pan for 20 minutes. Use the paper to lift them from the pan and transfer to a cooling rack to cool completely.

Cut into 16 squares.

FLAX

Though flax has had a meteoric rise in popularity since the 1950s, it is actually thought to have been in cultivation since 6000 BCE. And while its production long precedes its popularity, its modern uses are far tastier than its hippie cousins from the 1960s—I know I don't miss those dense, forty-pound loaves of flax-flecked whole wheat bread! Its nutty flavor adds so much complexity to dishes, while its texture adds crunch when coarsely ground, and both texture and body when finely ground. Try it finely ground in chocolate-specked muffins or light and fluffy homemade English muffins. I particularly love the nutty flavor flax adds to a smoothie: My favorite combo is flax, kale, and apple cider. And it's not just for eatin'—interestingly, the stalks of the plant were used to make mummy wrappings in ancient times and are still used today to create fine linens, baskets, and high-end artist paper.

Flax is a rich source of plant-based omega-3 fatty acids. Each tablespoon contains 1.8 grams of these "good" fats, and it is stuffed full of lignans, phytoestrogens that have seventy-five to eighty times more of both plant estrogen and antioxidant qualities than any other plant food. Now, let's talk about fiber: These tiny bundles are made up of 30 percent of both soluble and insoluble fiber. The oil from flax seeds—it's often labeled linseed oil—is a great source of polyunsaturated fatty acids, which along with other naturally occurring chemicals are purported to decrease inflammation.

TASTE, TEXTURE, APPEARANCE

Like chia, whole flax doesn't have a very distinctive flavor at the outset; grinding the seeds brings out their nutty flavor. Additionally, when the seeds are whole, their tough shells prevent them from breaking down in the intestines, which means their trove of vitamins and nutrients go unabsorbed. To get the most benefit from flax, whole seeds should be ground just before using. Whole seeds will yield almost twice as much when ground—a quarter cup of flax seeds will yield about a half cup of flax meal. Recipes calling for an exact amount of flax meal—typically baking recipes—will state the ground amount in the ingredient list. All other recipes where there is a little wiggle room will start with an amount of seeds, then ask for them to be ground.

BUYING AND KEEPING

You can find flax both as whole seeds or ground (aka flax meal). Both are available prepacked or in bulk, in grocery stores and online. The hard outer shells of whole flax seeds help keep them fresh a long time, so for best results grind the seeds as you need them. Store whole seeds in an airtight container, at room temperature, in a dark and cool place for six months, or refrigerate for one year. Flax meal should be stored in the refrigerator and stays fresh for up to six months. Store flax oil in the refrigerator for up to six months.

TOASTING INSTRUCTIONS

Toasting helps heighten the flavor of flax seeds. Toast the seeds in a medium sauté pan over low heat, stirring, until glistening and just starting to smell fragrant, 2 to 3 minutes, or in a 350°F oven, 8 to 10 minutes. For best results, toast seeds just before using.

flax and date milk

MAKES 3 CUPS

The dates give this milk a distinctively savory sweetness that perfectly complements flax's nuttiness. This milk is best served ice cold, so be sure to chill it completely before downing a tall glass. Store in an airtight container, in the refrigerator, for four days.

¼ cup toasted flax seeds
4 pitted dates
Kosher salt

Place the flax seeds and 3 cups of water in a bowl. Soak overnight in the refrigerator; drain.

Place the flax seeds, dates, a pinch of salt, and 3 cups of water in a blender. Blend on high until very smooth, 2 to 3 minutes.

Strain the milk through a nut milk bag or a very fine mesh metal strainer. Chill completely.

peanut flax butter

MAKES 1 CUP

Confession: I ate peanut butter and jelly sandwiches every day in high school. This is my adult version of PB—extra fiber and healthy fats from the flax, plus a nice hit of saltiness. Store in an airtight container, in the refrigerator, for two months.

2 cups roasted, unsalted peanuts
¼ cup toasted flax seeds, finely grated in a spice grinder
Kosher salt

Place the peanuts and flax seeds in a food processor. Process, stopping the food processor and scraping down the bowl as necessary, until the butter is smooth and creamy, 6 to 8 minutes. Season with salt.

TIP *Be patient when making nut butters. Six to 8 minutes in the food processor can seem like an eternity. The nuts will spin and spin, get grainy, continue to spin and spin, and eventually, with a little perseverance and belief, will become smooth. The time is worth the effort. The reward is a supersmooth and über-fresh nut butter.*

fall smoothie

MAKES 1 SERVING

This smoothie became a staple one fall when there was an excess of kale in the garden at the same time that the apples started falling from the trees. I picked kale by the truckload and made as much apple cider as I could handle. (The downside? Cleaning the juicer.) I always like to add protein to my smoothies—in this case, nut butter and flax seeds—so they keep me full. I can have one of these in the morning and not be hungry again until late afternoon!

2 packed cups torn kale leaves (about 4 leaves)

¾ cup apple cider

¼ cup Toasted Sunflower Seed and Almond Butter (page 149)

1 tablespoon toasted flax seeds, finely ground in a spice grinder

Place the kale, cider, sunflower almond butter, flax seeds, and ½ cup of ice in a blender.

Blend on high until very smooth, 30 seconds.

fiery watercress pesto

MAKES 1 CUP

Use watercress, not upland cress, in this spicy pesto. It's cheaper and bulkier and will yield a pesto that has a brighter green color. You can use any Manchego, but those that have been aged for at least six months will have a deeper, richer flavor than one aged only a month or two. This pesto is particularly delicious spooned over roasted cod or spread on toast and topped with sliced avocado and a sprinkling of flaky sea salt. Store in an airtight container, in the refrigerator, for five days.

1 cup finely chopped watercress

2 ounces Manchego, grated

1 tablespoon toasted flax seeds, finely ground in a spice grinder

1 small garlic clove

½ cup olive oil

Kosher salt

Place the watercress, Manchego, flax seeds, garlic, and ¼ cup of water in a blender. Blend on medium high, stopping the blender and scraping down the jar as necessary, until the mixture is almost smooth, 30 seconds to 1 minute. With the blender running, slowly add the oil through the feed tube. Process until the pesto is smooth, 10 to 20 seconds. Season with salt.

maple flax pecan shake

MAKES 1 CUP

As a southern girl, I love all things pecan, which makes this shake a real favorite. Try it in the morning on plain yogurt with chopped pear or apple or on the Mango Chia Pancakes (page 50). It's a wonderful alternative to maple syrup; you get the maple flavor, plus a little extra crunch from the pecans, without the cloying sweetness. Coarsely grind the flax seeds so that the shake maintains a nice loose texture. Store in an air-tight container, at room temperature, for up to two months.

¾ cup pecans

¼ cup toasted flax seeds, coarsely ground in a spice grinder

2 tablespoons maple sugar

Kosher salt

Preheat oven to 350°F. Spread the pecans on a small, rimmed baking sheet. Toast until just beginning to smell fragrant, 8 to 10 minutes. Finely chop.

Combine the pecans, flax seeds, maple sugar, and a pinch of salt in a bowl.

smoky white bean dip with parsley sauce

MAKES 4 SERVINGS

This dip is a fresh, homemade take on store-bought hummus that has chopped red pepper and oily herbs in the center. Serve with pita chips and flatbread for dipping or spread on a sandwich with thinly sliced salami, red onion, and crispy lettuce. The dip and sauce can be made up to one day ahead, but don't top the dip with the sauce until just before serving. And be sure to check the acidity level of the dip and topping before plating. Acid loses some of its oomph as it sits, so if it seems a little bland, stir in a few splashes of vinegar.

1 15.5-ounce can cannellini beans, drained and rinsed

⅓ cup plus 2 tablespoons olive oil, divided

3 teaspoons red wine vinegar, divided

1 garlic clove, chopped and divided

Kosher salt and freshly ground black pepper

½ cup fresh Italian parsley leaves, chopped

2 tablespoons chopped roasted almonds

2 teaspoons toasted flax seeds, finely ground in a spice grinder

½ teaspoon smoked paprika

Place the beans, ⅓ cup of olive oil, 2 teaspoons of vinegar, and ½ of the garlic clove in a food processor. Process until smooth. Season with salt and pepper.

Combine the parsley, almonds, flax seeds, paprika, remaining 2 tablespoons of oil, remaining teaspoon of vinegar, and remaining ½ garlic clove in a bowl. Season with salt and pepper.

Serve the dip topped with the parsley sauce.

> **TIP** *The green sauce on top of this dip has one of my favorite spices—smoked paprika. To maintain its freshness, store smoked paprika in the freezer for up to 2 months.*

rye and flax english muffins

MAKES 20 MUFFINS

These homemade English muffins are much lighter and fluffier than store-bought ones. These get their telltale sour flavor from cider vinegar, along with the unique flavor of rye flour. This dough is very wet, so be sure to liberally flour your hands when dividing the dough and shaping the muffins. To serve, split the muffins with a fork rather than slicing them with a knife; this will give you those classic nooks and crannies. Store in an airtight container, at room temperature, for two days, or freeze for one month.

4 cups bread flour, spooned and leveled, plus more for the work surface

1 cup rye flour, spooned and leveled

½ cup finely ground flax seeds

2 teaspoons kosher salt

3 tablespoons unsalted butter, melted, plus more for the bowl

1¾ cups whole milk, warmed to 100 to 110°F

1 package active dry yeast (¼ ounce)

1 large egg

2 tablespoons agave

4 teaspoons cider vinegar

¼ cup cornmeal

Whisk together the flours, flax seeds, and salt in a bowl. Rub the inside of a separate bowl with butter.

Pour the milk into a bowl and sprinkle in the yeast. Let sit until the yeast is bubbling, 5 to 7 minutes. If the yeast does not bubble, discard the mixture and start again. Whisk in the eggs, butter, agave, and vinegar.

Stir the dry ingredients into the wet ingredients until combined. Turn the dough out onto a floured work surface. Knead until the dough just comes together, 2 to 3 times.

Transfer the dough to the buttered bowl and turn to coat with the butter. Cover the bowl with a dishtowel and place it in a warm (but not hot) place. Let the dough rise until doubled in size, 1 hour to 2 hours.

Preheat oven to 350°F. Spread the cornmeal on the bottom of 2 rimmed baking sheets, dividing evenly.

With floured hands, divide the dough into 20 balls. Press each into a 3-inch hockey-puck-shaped disk. Place the disks on the prepared baking sheets and turn to lightly cover both sides in cornmeal.

Cover the sheets with dishtowels and place them in a warm (but not hot) place. Let the dough rise until slightly puffed, 30 to 40 minutes.

Heat a large nonstick sauté pan over medium heat. Cook the muffins, in batches, until golden-brown, 4 to 5 minutes per side (return to the baking sheets once browned). To cut down on time, when you get one sheet tray full of browned muffins, go ahead and pop it in the oven while you brown off the rest.

Bake until cooked through, 10 to 12 minutes.

TIP *A surefire way to tell if the muffins are done baking is to insert an instant-read thermometer in the center of one: It should register right around 200°F.*

banana buckwheat muffins

MAKES 12 MUFFINS

A coworker turned me on to the savory and sweet combo of buckwheat flour, banana, and chocolate, and I thank him for that! Buckwheat has a dark, intense flavor, so it's best to balance it with a lighter flour (in this case all-purpose). Because of the banana, these muffins stay moist and are really great warm— the chocolate chips will be melted and gooey. Reheat room temperature muffins in a 300°F oven for about five minutes. Store at room temperature, in an airtight container, for three days, or freeze for two weeks.

1 cup all-purpose flour, spooned and leveled

½ cup buckwheat flour, spooned and leveled

¼ cup finely ground flax seeds

½ teaspoon kosher salt

¼ teaspoon baking powder

¼ teaspoon baking soda

¼ cup whole milk

¼ cup (½ stick) unsalted butter, melted

¼ cup molasses

2 tablespoons light-brown sugar

1 large egg

⅔ cup mashed very ripe bananas (from 1 to 2 bananas)

¼ cup semisweet chocolate chips

1 tablespoon toasted sunflower seeds

Preheat oven to 350°F. Line a 12-cup standard muffin tin with liners.

Whisk together the flours, flax seeds, salt, baking powder, and baking soda in a bowl. Whisk together the milk, butter, molasses, sugar, and egg in a separate bowl. Whisk in the banana. Add the wet ingredients to the dry ingredients and stir to combine. Fold in the chocolate.

Divide the batter between the lined cups (about ¼ cup each). Top with the sunflower seeds. Bake, rotating the tins halfway, until a toothpick inserted in the center comes out clean, 25 to 30 minutes.

Set the tins on a wire rack and let the muffins cool in the pan for 10 minutes. After 10 minutes transfer the muffins to the wire rack.

Eat warm.

green salad with prosciutto and lemon flax dressing

MAKES 4 SERVINGS

A balanced salad is a beautiful thing and can make even the most devoted salad hater a lover. When perfectly constructed, a salad will have just the right amount of crunch, saltiness, and tang. The dressing for this salad is tart and sweet, making it a great match with salty prosciutto and crunchy vegetables. Store the dressing in an airtight container, in the refrigerator, for up to three days. As the dressing sits, the ground flax will make it thick. If necessary, thin with more oil or a little water before using.

¼ cup olive oil

2 tablespoons fresh lemon juice

1 tablespoon toasted flax seeds, coarsely ground

2 dates, finely chopped

Kosher salt and freshly ground black pepper

½ bunch asparagus, trimmed and cut into 3-inch pieces

1 small head Bibb lettuce, leaves torn

½ small head frisée, leaves torn

1 Persian cucumber, sliced

½ shallot, thinly sliced

⅓ cup toasted hulled pumpkin seeds (see page 180)

2 ounces prosciutto, torn

Whisk together the oil, lemon juice, flax seeds, and dates in a bowl. Season with salt and pepper.

Cook the asparagus in a medium saucepan of boiling salted water until crisp tender, 1 to 3 minutes. Drain and run under cold water to cool. Pat dry with paper towels.

Toss together the dressing, asparagus, Bibb lettuce, frisée, cucumber, shallot, pumpkin seeds, and prosciutto. Season with salt and pepper.

briny tomato and chicken panzanella

MAKES 4 SERVINGS

Panzanella, a classic Italian dish, combines the best of what's around during the hot summer months (tomatoes galore!) and what's often in the back corner of the kitchen cupboard—stale bread. In this case, the recipe uses the Rye and Flax English Muffins, which adds a great layer of flavor. There are three options for preparing the muffins for this recipe: (1) Simply forget about them and they go stale. (2) Tear them up into bite-sized pieces and let them sit out, uncovered, at room temperature for a few days. (3) Tear them up into bite-sized pieces, toss with a little oil, and toast until dry and golden. Though it's not classical, this recipe directs you to take option 3, but feel free to choose your own adventure.

2 bone-in, skin-on chicken thighs

1 sprig fresh rosemary

2 garlic cloves, smashed

7 tablespoons olive oil, divided

Kosher salt and freshly ground black pepper

4 Rye and Flax English Muffins (page 72), torn into bite-sized pieces

1½ pounds mixed tomatoes, cut into bite-sized pieces

3 tablespoons red wine vinegar

1 bunch arugula, torn

⅓ cup Kalamata olives, halved

¼ cup toasted sunflower seeds

¼ cup chopped fresh chives

1 tablespoon capers

> TIP *No grill? Roast the thighs in a 425°F oven for 25 to 30 minutes.*

Combine the chicken, rosemary, garlic, and 1 tablespoon of the oil in a bowl. Season with salt and pepper. Marinate in the refrigerator for at least 1 hour and up to 24 hours.

Heat grill to medium high and set up for indirect grilling (see page 9 for tips). Discard the rosemary and garlic. Grill the chicken over indirect heat, covered, turning once, until cooked through, 25 to 30 minutes. Cool completely. Discard the skin and bone. Shred the chicken.

Preheat oven to 350°F. Toss together the English muffins and 2 tablespoons of the oil. Season with salt and pepper. Toast on a rimmed baking sheet until golden-brown and crispy, 14 to 16 minutes.

Toss together the toasted English muffins, tomatoes, vinegar, and remaining 4 tablespoons of oil in a bowl. Let sit, stirring occasionally, until the English muffins start to absorb some of the liquid, 4 to 6 minutes.

Add the shredded chicken, arugula, olives, sunflower seeds, chives, and capers to the tomato mixture and toss to combine. Season with salt and pepper.

cauliflower and cabbage gratin

MAKES 6 TO 8 SERVINGS

This is a twist on the well-known potatoes gratin. Cauliflower and cabbage replace the potatoes, get coated in a creamy béchamel sauce, and baked with a crunchy flax-coated breadcrumb topping. The typically all whole milk béchamel is lightened up by using half whole milk and half vegetable stock. (You can also use chicken stock if you have it on hand.) Serve this creamy side with steak, whole roasted chicken, or even alongside turkey at Thanksgiving. Store the uncooked gratin, covered, in the refrigerator, for up to one day. Bring to room temperature and bake as instructed.

4 tablespoons unsalted butter, plus more for the tinfoil

1 small head cauliflower, cut into medium florets

Kosher salt and freshly ground black pepper

½ cup all-purpose flour, spooned and leveled

1½ cups whole milk

1½ cups vegetable stock (page 204)

4 ounces sharp Cheddar, grated

¼ head savoy cabbage, halved and sliced into 1½-inch pieces

8 ounces sourdough bread, torn into bite-sized pieces

2 tablespoons olive oil

2 tablespoons toasted flax seeds, coarsely ground

Preheat oven to 350°F. Rub one side of a large piece of tinfoil with butter.

Cook the cauliflower in a medium saucepan of boiling salted water until crisp tender, 6 to 8 minutes. Drain.

Melt the butter in a medium saucepan over medium heat. Add the flour and cook, whisking constantly, for 30 seconds (this cooks off the flour flavor). Slowly whisk in the milk, then the stock. Bring to a boil then reduce to a simmer. Cook, stirring often, until thickened, 8 to 10 minutes. Remove from the heat and stir in the Cheddar until melted. Stir in the cauliflower and cabbage. Season with salt and pepper. Transfer the vegetables and all of the sauce to a 2-quart baking dish.

Toss together the bread, oil, and flax seeds in a bowl. Season with salt and pepper. Top the cauliflower mixture with the breadcrumbs.

Tightly cover the dish with the prepared foil. Bake until the sauce is bubbling, 18 to 20 minutes. Uncover and bake until the breadcrumbs are brown and crispy, 14 to 16 minutes.

Let rest 5 minutes before serving.

TIP *To test that your béchamel is the proper consistency, coat the back of a wooden spoon with sauce then run your finger through it. If the line doesn't fill in then—voilà!—it's ready.*

cod fillets with saucy braised leeks

MAKES 4 SERVINGS

Now that I live in the South, I find myself needing to balance the rich, often fried, dinners that are staples in these parts with healthier options. These light, meal-coated fish fillets served with buttery braised leeks and fresh spring spinach perfectly fit the bill. The topping for the fish needs very little oil because the natural oil from the ground pine nuts helps hold the coating together. The topping can be made, and the fish coated, up to eight hours in advance. Store, tightly wrapped, in the refrigerator.

¼ cup pine nuts

1 tablespoon flax seeds, finely ground in a spice grinder

1 tablespoon olive oil

2 teaspoons fresh thyme leaves

Kosher salt and freshly ground black pepper

2 tablespoons unsalted butter

4 small leeks (white and light green parts), halved

1 cup chicken stock (page 203)

¼ cup dry white wine (such as sauvignon blanc)

4 6- to 8-ounce cod fillets

3 packed cups baby spinach

TIP *Save and freeze the dark green parts of the leeks for making stock.*

Preheat oven to 350°F. Spread the pine nuts on a small baking sheet. Toast until light golden-brown, 6 to 8 minutes. Finely grind in a spice grinder. Combine the ground pine nuts, flax seeds, oil, and thyme in a bowl. Season with salt and pepper.

Increase oven temperature to 425°F.

Melt the butter in a large straight-sided sauté pan over medium-high heat. Add the leeks, cut-side down. Season with salt and pepper. Cook until golden-brown, 3 to 5 minutes. Flip and cook until brown on the second side, 3 to 5 minutes.

Add the stock and wine. Simmer, covered, until the leeks are tender, 10 to 12 minutes.

While the leeks are simmering, cook the fish. Season the cod with salt and pepper. Place on a rimmed baking sheet and top with the nut mixture. Roast until just opaque throughout, 14 to 16 minutes.

Stir the spinach into the leeks.

Serve the fish over the vegetables with any liquid from the pan.

caramelized onion and fennel quiche with flax-speckled crust

This quiche is light on eggs but heavy on cream, so it is incredibly rich—a small piece goes a long way. The flax seeds make the crust very tender and give it a deep flavor and color, while the long-cooked onion and fennel take on a deeper caramel flavor. The dough can be made, and the onion and fennel browned, up to two days in advance; store both, tightly wrapped, in the refrigerator. The finished dish will keep three days, but the bottom crust will start to get a little soft. So if you are serving for guests, make it the day of.

1 cup all-purpose flour, spooned and leveled, plus more for the work surface

¼ cup finely ground flax seeds

Kosher salt and freshly ground black pepper

½ cup plus 3 tablespoons cold unsalted butter, cut up, divided

1 medium yellow onion, chopped

1 small fennel bulb, chopped

4 large eggs

1 cup heavy cream

¾ cup whole milk

Pinch freshly grated nutmeg

3 ounces Gruyère, grated (about ¾ cup)

Place the flour, flax seeds, and 1 teaspoon of salt in a food processor. Pulse until combined. Add the ½ cup of butter and pulse until the butter is broken into pea-size pieces. Drizzle with 3 tablespoons of ice-cold water and pulse to incorporate. The dough should not form a ball in the machine, but it should hold together when squeezed. If it doesn't hold together, add up to 1 more tablespoon of water and pulse to incorporate. Transfer the dough to a large piece of plastic wrap. Use the plastic wrap to bring the dough together into a ball; flatten into a disk. Refrigerate until firm, at least 30 minutes or up to two days.

While the dough is chilling, caramelize the onion and fennel. Melt the remaining 3 tablespoons of butter in a medium skillet over medium heat. Add the onion and fennel. Season with salt and pepper. Cook, stirring occasionally, until deep brown in color, 40 to 45 minutes (reduce the heat to medium low if the onions start to burn). Cool to room temperature.

Preheat oven to 350°F with the oven rack in the lowest position.

(continued) ▶

Remove the dough from the plastic wrap and place onto a liberally floured work surface. With a floured rolling pin, roll the dough to a 15-inch circle. Fit the dough into the bottom and sides of a 9-inch springform pan (the dough won't come all the way up the sides). Refrigerate until chilled, at least 1 hour.

Whisk together the eggs in a bowl. Add the browned onion and fennel, cream, milk, nutmeg, 1 teaspoon of salt, and ½ teaspoon of pepper and whisk to combine.

Sprinkle the Gruyère on the bottom of the chilled crust. Pour the egg mixture on top.

Place the pan on a rimmed baking sheet. Bake until the filling is firm around the edges and just slightly wobbly in the center, 1 hour to 1 hour 10 minutes.

Let rest for 10 minutes before releasing the sides of the springform pan and slicing the quiche.

TIP *Be sure to chill the crust completely before adding the filling; this will ensure it doesn't flop over when baking. Pop it in the freezer for fifteen minutes if you're in a rush.*

FLAX

toasted farro with flax-coated carrots and scallions

MAKES 4 TO 6 SERVINGS

I eat grains topped with myriad roasted vegetables for dinner and lunch several times a week. It's so easy to make large batches of both, and because they reheat really well (but are also great at room temp—bonus!), they are perfect for leftovers. And amazingly, almost any combination works. Part of what makes this meal so delicious is the toppings—so don't skimp! I have listed my favorites but give fresh salsa, guacamole, sour cream, goat cheese, or feta a try. Store in an airtight container, in the refrigerator, for up to five days.

1 pound carrots, halved lengthwise

8 scallions, white and light green parts left whole, plus ½ cup sliced dark green parts

2 tablespoons flax seeds, coarsely ground

1½ teaspoons cumin seeds

6 tablespoons olive oil, divided

Kosher salt and freshly ground black pepper

1 cup farro

1 sprig fresh oregano

1 15.5-ounce black beans, drained and rinsed

1 cup fresh cilantro leaves and tender stems, chopped

¼ cup toasted sunflower seeds

1 teaspoon finely grated lime zest, plus 2 tablespoons lime juice

Queso fresco, for serving

Preheat oven to 450°F.

Toss together the carrots, scallion whites, flax seeds, cumin seeds, and 2 tablespoons of the oil. Season with salt and pepper. Roast on a rimmed baking sheet, tossing once, until the carrots are golden-brown and tender, 20 to 25 minutes.

While the carrots roast, cook the *farro*. Heat a medium saucepan over medium-high heat for 30 seconds. Add 1 tablespoon of the oil and heat for 10 seconds. Add the *farro* and oregano. Cook, stirring occasionally, until the *farro* is darkened and smells toasty, 4 to 5 minutes. Cover with water and simmer until the *farro* is tender, 18 to 20 minutes. Drain and shake to remove as much of the water as possible. Discard the oregano. Return the *farro* to the pot and stir in the beans.

Combine the cilantro, sunflower seeds, lime zest, lime juice, scallion greens, and the remaining 3 tablespoon of oil in a bowl. Season with salt and pepper.

Serve the vegetables over the *farro* drizzled with the cilantro dressing and topped with *queso fresco*.

carrot and beef meatballs with marinara

MAKES 4 SERVINGS

I love to break from tradition and dish up spaghetti and meatballs for Christmas dinner, but this meal can really be served any time you're craving something hearty. These tender meatballs are packed full of parsley, carrots, and fiber-rich flax—though you wouldn't know it by their luxurious taste. Browning the meatballs, then finishing them in the sauce, helps all the flavors meld. Store the uncooked meatballs in an airtight container, in the refrigerator, for up to one day.

1 pound 85 percent lean ground beef

2 small carrots, grated

½ cup fresh Italian parsley leaves, finely chopped

¼ cup finely ground flax seeds

3 ounces Parmesan, grated, plus more for serving

1 large egg

4 garlic cloves, finely chopped, divided

Kosher salt and freshly ground black pepper

3 tablespoons olive oil

½ yellow onion, chopped

1 28-ounce can whole peeled tomatoes

¾ pound spaghetti

Gently combine the beef, carrots, parsley, flax seeds, Parmesan, egg, and 2 cloves of the garlic in a bowl. Season with 1 teaspoon salt and ¼ teaspoon pepper. Shape the mixture into 12 meatballs (about 2 tablespoons each).

Heat a large straight-sided sauté pan over medium-high heat for 30 seconds. Add the oil and heat for 10 seconds. Add the meatballs. Cook, turning occasionally, until brown on all sides, 7 to 9 minutes (they won't be cooked all the way through). Transfer to a plate.

Pour off all but 2 tablespoons of the fat in the pan. Add the onion and the remaining 2 garlic cloves to the pan. Season with salt and pepper. Cook, stirring, until the onion is tender, 3 to 4 minutes.

Add the tomatoes. Season with salt and pepper. Simmer, breaking up the tomatoes with a spoon, until the sauce is slightly thickened, 4 to 5 minutes.

Return the browned meatballs to the pan. Gently simmer until the meatballs are cooked through and the sauce is thickened, 18 to 20 minutes.

While the meatballs cook, boil the pasta. Bring a large pot of salted water to a boil. Add pasta and cook according to package directions until al dente.

Serve the pasta topped with the sauce, meatballs, and grated Parmesan.

baked puddings with boozy caramel sauce

MAKES 4 SERVINGS

These puddings are based on a traditional English dessert—think of a super-moist, rich cake topped with a dark (and slightly boozy!) caramel sauce. For incredibly tender puddings, finely grate the carrots with a Microplane, and don't stop processing the prunes until they are finely chopped. (If you don't have a Microplane, use the smallest holes on a box grater.) Serve the puddings either in the ramekins they bake in—poke a few holes in them with a toothpick and pour the sauce on the top—or turn them out onto a plate. Make the caramel sauce up to three days in advance. Store in an airtight container in the refrigerator.

5 tablespoons unsalted butter, at room temperature, divided, plus more for ramekins

1 cup pitted prunes

⅔ cup all-purpose flour, spooned and leveled

⅓ cup ground flax seeds

½ teaspoon baking powder

¼ teaspoon baking soda

½ teaspoon kosher salt

¼ cup packed dark-brown sugar

1 large egg

1 teaspoon pure vanilla extract

½ cup finely grated carrot (from 1 medium carrot)

½ cup granulated sugar

¼ cup heavy cream

1 tablespoon brandy

Preheat oven to 350°F. Butter 4 6-ounce ramekins. Place the ramekins on a baking sheet.

Soak the prunes in ⅓ cup warm water until very soft, 14 to 16 minutes. Transfer the prunes and liquid to a food processor. Process until finely chopped, 30 seconds to 1 minute.

While the prunes are soaking, make the batter. Whisk together the flour, flax seeds, baking powder, baking soda, and salt in a bowl.

Beat the brown sugar and 4 tablespoons of the butter with an electric mixer on medium-high speed until light and fluffy, 2 to 3 minutes. Add the egg and beat until fully incorporated. Add the vanilla and beat to combine. Reduce the mixer speed to low and gradually beat in the flour mixture. Add the prunes and carrot and beat to combine. Transfer the batter to the buttered ramekins, dividing evenly. Bake, until a toothpick inserted in the center comes out with a few crumbs attached, 24 to 26 minutes.

(continued) ▶

▶ *Baked Puddings with Boozy Caramel Sauce* (continued)

While the puddings are baking, make the caramel sauce. Combine the granulated sugar and 2 tablespoons water in a small saucepan. Cook over medium-high heat, stirring, until the sugar is combined, 1 to 3 minutes. Once the sugar has melted, stop stirring and simmer, until it turns dark golden-brown, 8 to 10 minutes. Remove the saucepan from the heat and add the cream carefully; the mixture will sputter. Once the mixture has stopped sputtering, swirl in the brandy, remaining tablespoon of butter, and a pinch of salt.

Serve the sauce over the warm puddings.

TIP *Most sauté pans tend to cook unevenly, which often leads to the caramel getting a dark spot before turning golden-brown overall. If this happens, give the saucepan a quick swirl to incorporate it.*

parmesan popcorn with a kick

MAKES 4 SERVINGS

This is very savory popcorn—the Parm gives it a low, umami flavor, while ample amounts of black pepper adds a spicy kick. Use a Microplane to very finely grate the cheese and be sure to toss the popcorn with the toppings as soon as it comes out of the pan; this will give the cheese a chance to melt. Though all of it won't melt, trust me: Everyone will be fighting over the goodies in the bottom of the bowl. If you can find an heirloom variety of popcorn, grab it! The kernels are typically much smaller than commercial brands but have a ton more flavor and better texture.

4 tablespoons canola oil
½ cup popcorn kernels
2 tablespoons finely ground flax seeds
1 ounce Parmesan, very finely grated
1 tablespoon olive oil
Kosher salt and freshly ground black pepper

Heat the canola oil and one popcorn kernel in a covered, medium saucepan over medium-high heat. Once the kernel has popped, add the remaining kernels. Cook, covered, until the kernels start popping vigorously. Lower the heat to medium and open the lid slightly to allow the steam to release (but not enough to let the popping kernels fly out!). Cook until there are 2 to 3 seconds between pops. Remove from the heat and let stand for 30 seconds.

Toss the popcorn with the flax seeds, Parmesan, and olive oil. Season with salt and a generous amount of pepper.

cinnamon sandwich cookies with fresh raspberry filling

I love to serve these pretty little cookies with tea or a cup of afternoon coffee. They are delicious filled with the fresh raspberry filling or on their own. Don't make the sandwiches until just before serving because the filling will make the cookies soggy and cause them to crumble. Make the dough and filling up to two days in advance; store both, tightly wrapped, in the refrigerator.

1 cup all-purpose flour, spooned and leveled

½ cup almond flour, spooned and leveled

¼ cup finely ground flax seeds

½ teaspoon ground cinnamon

½ teaspoon plus a pinch kosher salt, divided

½ cup (1 stick) unsalted butter, at room temperature

¼ cup packed light-brown sugar

1 large egg yolk

½ teaspoon pure vanilla extract

2 teaspoons cornstarch

½ cup fresh raspberries

3 tablespoons confectioners' sugar

¼ teaspoon finely grated lemon zest

Whisk together the flours, ground flax seeds, cinnamon, and salt in a bowl.

Beat the butter and brown sugar with an electric mixer on medium-high speed until light and fluffy, 2 to 3 minutes. Add the egg yolk and beat until fully incorporated. Add the vanilla and beat to combine. Reduce the mixer speed to low and gradually beat in the flour mixture until fully incorporated. Transfer the dough to a large piece of parchment and roll into a 1¼-inch thick log. Refrigerate until very firm, at least 2 hours and up to 1 day.

Preheat oven to 350°F. Line 2 rimmed baking sheets with parchment.

Using a serrated knife cut the log into ⅜-inch-thick cookies and place them 1 inch apart on the lined baking sheets. Bake, rotating the sheets front to back and top to bottom halfway through, until golden-brown, 11 to 12 minutes.

Cool the cookies on the baking sheets for 5 minutes then transfer to a cooling rack to cool completely.

While the dough is chilling and the cookies are baking, make the raspberry filling. Whisk together the cornstarch and 1 tablespoon water in a small saucepan until the cornstarch is dissolved. Add the raspberries, confectioners' sugar, lemon zest, and a pinch of salt. Mash with a potato masher until the raspberries are broken down. Cook over medium heat, stirring, until thickened, 1 to 2 minutes. Chill completely.

Top half of the cookies with the filling (about ½ teaspoon each) and sandwich with the remaining cookies.

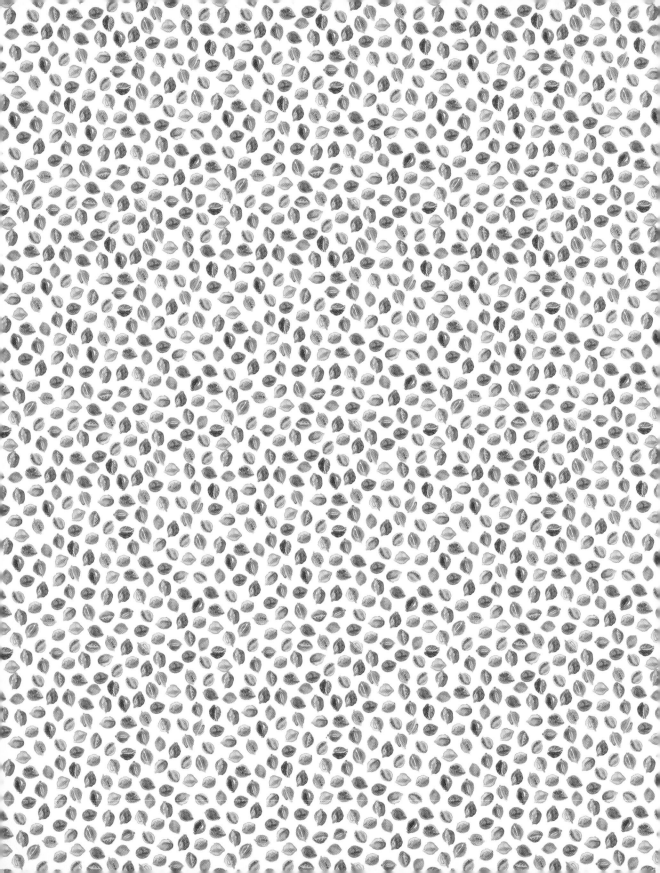

HEMP

don't believe most people knew that hemp seeds were edible until recently. The plant was forever negatively associated with tote bags and roughly textured clothing. In fact, hemp was first brought to North America in the early seventeenth century, and since then, its fibers have been used to make paper (like that used to draft the Declaration of Independence), sails, cloth, and rope—the list goes on and on.

In recent decades, the growing interest in superfoods has sparked a grocery store frenzy, giving these little gems prime real estate on aisle endcaps. Once I started cooking with hemp seeds, I quickly got in the habit of throwing them into everything. A dash in a morning smoothie, sprinkled in a grilled cheese sandwich, or mixed with herbs and spices for a delicious stew topping.

Contrary to popular belief, you won't get a buzz from eating hemp seeds. Hemp grown for food contains less than 1 percent, or virtually no, THC—the compound in marijuana that makes one "high." And because the US government severely restricts the cultivation of hemp, most hemp consumed in the US is imported.

Hemp contains all of the essential amino acids to fuel the human body, making it a great source of vegan protein. It is also high in dietary fiber, essential fatty acids (omega-3 and omega-6), antioxidants, vitamins, and minerals. Hemp provides an abundance of energy, stabilizes the appetite, and improves one's digestion.

Unrefined hemp oil is purported to have the least amount of unsaturated fat of any plant-derived oil. It has an amazing emerald color and an intensely nutty flavor, with a hint of grassiness. Both the plant and seeds can be pressed to produce the oil. Once refined, the oil loses most of its color and flavor. Use the oil in small quantities in sauces or dressings (I love it in pesto)—too much can be overpowering—and don't cook with it as it easily burns.

TASTE, TEXTURE, APPEARANCE

Hulled hemp seeds are called hemp hearts, and they have a slightly waxy texture and a mild nutty flavor that becomes much more pronounced when toasted. Hemp seeds are small, about the size of a pinhead, and range in color from off-white to green to black. When ground, hemp seeds become sticky and tend to clump up into a ball, so be sure to break up ground seeds before adding them to a recipe.

BUYING AND KEEPING

You can find hemp seeds packaged or in bulk at grocery stores and in health-food stores. You can also purchase them online. Unopened containers of hemp seeds can be stored at room temperature for two months. Once opened, refrigerate for up to one year, or freeze for one and a half years. Store hemp oil in the refrigerator for up to three months.

TOASTING INSTRUCTIONS

Toasting hemp really brings out its rich flavor and changes the texture from waxy to crunchy. Toast in a medium sauté pan over medium heat, stirring until light golden-brown and fragrant, 3 to 5 minutes.

hemp milk

MAKES 3 CUPS

This is my favorite seed milk; I really love how the flavor of the seeds pairs perfectly with the rich vanilla. It's particularly delicious with granola or over oatmeal. Store in an airtight container, in the refrigerator, for one week.

1 cup hemp seeds

1 tablespoon agave

1 teaspoon pure vanilla extract

Kosher salt

Place the hemp seeds and 3 cups of water in a bowl. Soak overnight in the refrigerator; drain.

Place the hemp seeds, agave, vanilla, a pinch of salt, and 3 cups of water in a blender. Blend on high until very smooth, 2 to 3 minutes.

Strain the milk through a nut milk bag or a very fine mesh metal strainer. Chill completely.

mango citrus smoothie

MAKES 1 SERVING

This beautiful yellow smoothie gets its creamy texture from the mango, with a bright fresh flavor from the lime zest and mint. Using hemp seeds and milk gives it a big protein boost, making it a great way to start the day or as a midafternoon snack to keep you going until dinner. Feel free to substitute fresh peeled mango for frozen. Add a half-cup of ice to chill.

1¼ cups frozen mango chunks

¾ cup Hemp Milk (page 95)

2 tablespoons fresh mint leaves

2 tablespoons hemp seeds

½ teaspoon lime zest

Place the mango, hemp milk, mint, hemp seeds, and lime zest in a blender. Blend on high until very smooth, 30 seconds.

chocolate hazelnut hemp butter

MAKES 2⅓ CUPS

I first discovered Nutella when my family moved to Italy when I was in third grade. This healthier (less sugar) homemade version is not completely smooth—think of it more like a natural peanut butter versus Jif. If you're wed to a perfectly smooth spread, you can strain it through a fine mesh sieve. (Straining will reduce the yield to about one and one half cups.) Store in an airtight container, at room temperature, for two months.

2 cups hazelnuts

1 cup toasted hemp seeds

¼ cup Dutch-processed cocoa powder

¼ cup confectioners' sugar

1 teaspoon pure vanilla extract

6 ounces semisweet chocolate, melted

Kosher salt

Preheat oven to 350°F. Spread the hazelnuts on a small, rimmed baking sheet. Toast, until just beginning to smell fragrant, 10 to 12 minutes. Rub the nuts in a clean dishtowel to remove the skins (don't worry if a few of the skins are still attached).

Place the skinned hazelnuts, hemp seeds, cocoa powder, sugar, and vanilla in a food processor. Process, stopping the food processor and scraping down the bowl as necessary, until the butter is smooth and creamy, 4 to 6 minutes. Add the melted chocolate. Process until combined, 1 to 2 minutes. Season with salt.

hemp and parsley pesto

MAKES 1 CUP

Using hemp oil in this pesto adds another layer of nutty goodness. Don't worry if you don't have it, though; simply use all olive oil. I love this pesto spooned over roasted chicken and garlicky potatoes, and I often find myself eating it drizzled over tomatoes alongside sliced cheese and a few crackers for a quick dinner or snack. Store in an airtight container, in the refrigerator, for five days.

¼ cup toasted hemp seeds
2 ounces Pecorino, grated
1 garlic clove
2 packed cups fresh Italian parsley leaves
¼ cup olive oil
2 tablespoons hemp oil
Kosher salt and freshly ground black pepper

Place the hemp seeds, Pecorino, and garlic in a blender. Blend on medium high until finely chopped, 20 seconds. Add the parsley and ½ cup of water. Blend on medium high, stopping the blender and scraping down the jar as necessary, until the mixture is almost smooth, about 1 minute. With the blender running, slowly add the oils through the feed tube. Process until the pesto is smooth, about 20 seconds. Season with salt and pepper.

hemp and red pepper shake

MAKES ¼ CUP

Floral notes from the coriander and a touch of spice from the red pepper flakes make this shake great on grilled vegetables or sprinkled on raw fish before searing or roasting. Use a spice grinder or mortar and pestle to crush the bay leaf as finely as possible. Store in an airtight container, at room temperature, for two months.

¼ cup toasted hemp seeds
1 tablespoon crushed coriander seeds
1 small bay leaf, finely crushed
½ teaspoon red pepper flakes
Kosher salt

Combine the hemp seeds, coriander seeds, bay leaf, and red pepper flakes. Season with salt.

lemony red pepper dip

MAKES 1½ CUPS

Textured, intensely colorful, and tangy, this dip is excellent served with toasted pita or flatbread. Look for preserved lemons (lemons that have been cured in salt and lemon juice) in specialty markets or Middle Eastern stores or order them online. They are also simple to make, although they have to sit for several weeks before they can be used—so plan ahead. Make the dip up to one day in advance, but don't stir in the vinegar until just before serving.

2 red bell peppers

½ cup pitted green olives, chopped

2 tablespoons toasted hemp seeds

1 tablespoon capers, chopped

1 tablespoon finely chopped preserved lemon

¼ cup olive oil

2 tablespoons red wine vinegar

Kosher salt and freshly ground black pepper

Toast the peppers directly over two burners of a gas stove, set to high, or under a broiler, turning often, until black all over, 8 to 10 minutes. Transfer to a bowl and cover with a piece of foil and allow to cool completely. Once cool, discard the blackened skin, seeds, and stem; coarsely chop.

Combine the peppers, olives, hemp seeds, capers, preserved lemon, oil, and vinegar in a bowl. Season with salt and pepper.

toasted cashew, coconut, and molasses granola

MAKES 5 CUPS

Tart dried cherries—a delicious though expensive ingredient—pair perfectly with the coconut and cinnamon in this granola. If you don't feel like shelling out the bucks for dried cherries, feel free to substitute chopped dried figs or apricots. Try this granola for dessert sprinkled over ice cream or tossed with roasted winter squash. Store in an airtight container, at room temperature, for one month.

½ cup sweetened coconut

3 cups old-fashioned rolled oats

1 cup raw cashews, chopped

⅓ cup raw hemp seeds

2 teaspoons ground cinnamon

1 teaspoon kosher salt

⅓ cup molasses

4 tablespoons unsalted butter, melted

½ cup dried cherries

Preheat oven to 325°F.

Spread the coconut on a small, rimmed baking sheet. Toast, stirring often, until golden-brown, 10 to 12 minutes.

While the coconut is toasting, combine the oats, cashews, hemp seeds, cinnamon, and salt in a bowl. Add the molasses and butter and stir until everything is evenly coated. Spread the granola on a large, rimmed baking sheet. Bake, stirring twice, until the oats and cashews are toasted, 18 to 20 minutes.

Combine the granola, toasted coconut, and cherries in a bowl.

seeded apricot and pecan crackers

MAKES 48 CRACKERS

These crackers are made using the same technique as that for biscotti (the batter is baked then thinly sliced and crisped). They are savory with a slightly sweet note—which makes them excellent with a smear of fresh goat cheese and a drizzle of olive oil or salty olive tapenade. Store in an airtight container, at room temperature, for two weeks. If they get soft, spread them on a baking sheet and toast at 250°F until crisp again.

Unsalted butter, for baking dish

1 cup all-purpose flour, spooned and leveled

1 cup whole wheat flour, spooned and leveled

2 teaspoons baking powder

2 teaspoons kosher salt

1 cup dried apricots, chopped

¾ cup pecans, chopped

½ cup hulled pumpkin seeds

¼ cup hemp seeds

¼ cup hulled sesame seeds

2 tablespoons dark-brown sugar

1 cup full-fat vanilla yogurt

1 cup whole milk

Preheat oven to 325°F. Butter an 8-inch square baking dish. Line 2 rimmed baking sheets with parchment.

Whisk together the flours, baking powder, and salt in a bowl. Add the apricots, pecans, pumpkin seeds, hemp seeds, sesame seeds, and sugar and stir to combine. Add the yogurt and milk and stir until the batter comes together. Pour the batter into the prepared baking dish. Bake until a toothpick inserted in the center comes out clean, 35 to 45 minutes. Let cool for 15 minutes. Remove the cake from the pan and transfer to a wire rack to cool completely.

Using a long serrated knife, cut the edges off all four sides of the cake; discard. Cut the cake into quarters through the middle. Working with one quarter at a time, thinly slice into crackers. Transfer to the prepared baking sheets and bake, in 2 batches if necessary, rotating the pans and flipping the crackers halfway through, until browned and crisp, 20 to 30 minutes. Transfer to a wire rack to cool completely.

TIP *For the crispiest crackers, slice them as thinly as possible—¼ inch is ideal.*

overnight waffles
with caramelized peaches

These waffles are reminiscent of sourdough bread. The yeasted batter sits overnight, taking on a slight tang from the fermentation, and is ready to cook up as soon as you wake in the morning. Perfect for a weekend with houseguests! Serve with whatever you like to eat waffles with—yogurt, maple syrup, or crème fraîche—and try them in the winter months with pears or apples instead of peaches.

1¾ cups all-purpose flour, spooned and leveled

½ cup white whole wheat flour

¼ cup toasted hemp seeds

1 teaspoon kosher salt

2 cups whole milk, warmed to 100 to 110°F

3 tablespoons sugar, divided

1 package active dry yeast (¼ ounce)

3 tablespoons unsalted butter, divided

1 vanilla bean

4 firm but ripe peaches, pitted and each cut into 8 wedges

2 large eggs

¼ teaspoon baking soda

TIP *When you caramelize the peaches, don't flip them until they get nice and brown on the first side; this may require rotating the sauté pan around the burner so they cook evenly.*

The night before, whisk together the flours, hemp seeds, and salt in a bowl.

Combine the milk and 1 tablespoon of the sugar in a measuring cup. Sprinkle the yeast on top of the milk. Let sit until the yeast is bubbling, 5 to 7 minutes (if the yeast does not bubble, discard the mixture and start again). Melt 2 tablespoons of the butter and whisk into the yeast mixture.

Add the wet ingredients to the dry ingredients and stir to combine. Cover and let sit 8 hours or up to overnight, in a cool spot (either on the kitchen counter, or if you prefer, in the fridge), until bubbly.

When you're ready to prepare the waffles, halve the vanilla bean lengthwise and scrape the seeds from the inside. Use your fingers to distribute the seeds in the remaining 2 tablespoons of sugar in a bowl. Melt the remaining tablespoon of butter in a large nonstick sauté pan over medium-high heat. Sprinkle the sugar on the butter then top with the peaches, cut-side down. Cook, until golden-brown on one side, 5 to 7 minutes. Flip and cook until soft throughout, 1 to 2 minutes. Transfer to a bowl and cover to keep warm.

Preheat oven to 200°F. Place a baking sheet inside.

Add the eggs and baking soda to the waffle batter and whisk to combine. Cook the waffles according to the instructions for your waffle machine, transferring them to the baking sheet in the oven to keep warm.

Serve the waffles with the caramelized peaches.

cheddar hemp scones

Tall, buttery, and flaky—everything you want in a scone. Eat them warm, right out of the oven, or cool and freeze for up to two weeks. Bring frozen scones to room temperature then gently reheat in a 300°F oven. To serve, go "sweet and savory," slather them with jam, or gild the lily and serve with pats of butter or crispy bacon.

2 cups all-purpose flour, spooned and leveled, plus more for work surface

¼ cup toasted hemp seeds

1 tablespoon baking powder

1½ teaspoons kosher salt

6 tablespoons cold unsalted butter, cut-up

4 ounces Cheddar cheese, grated

¾ cup plus 2 tablespoons buttermilk

Preheat oven to 425°F. Line a baking sheet with parchment.

Whisk together the flour, hemp seeds, baking powder, and salt in a bowl. Add the butter and use the tips of your fingers to break it into pea-sized pieces. Add the Cheddar and stir twice to combine. Add the buttermilk and stir until the dough comes together.

Turn the dough out onto a floured work surface. Form the dough into a 6½-inch by 1-inch-thick circle. Cut into 8 wedges; transfer to the baking sheet. Bake until golden-brown and cooked through, 20 to 24 minutes.

cherry and pistachio grain salad

MAKES 4 SERVINGS

This is my favorite type of salad because it's healthful, filling, sweet, salty, and crunchy. Try substituting the cherries with chopped peaches or nectarines, and during winter months, pomegranate seeds. The *farro* can be made three days ahead, but don't toss with the remaining ingredients until just before serving.

**Kosher salt and freshly ground
  black pepper**

1 cup farro

1 cup halved and pitted fresh cherries

⅓ cup roasted pistachios, chopped

¼ cup fresh basil leaves, torn

**2 ounces Gruyère, cut into small
  pieces**

1 small shallot, chopped

2 tablespoons toasted hemp seeds

2 tablespoons fresh lemon juice

2 tablespoons olive oil

Bring a small saucepan of salted water to a boil. Add the *farro* and simmer until just tender, 25 to 30 minutes. Drain and run under cold water to cool completely. Shake to remove as much water as possible. Spread the grains on a small baking sheet or plate and refrigerate, stirring once, until the grains are completely dry, 30 minutes.

Combine the grains, cherries, pistachios, basil, Gruyère, shallot, hemp seeds, lemon juice, and oil in a bowl. Season with salt and pepper.

toasted brown rice pilaf

This classic French side dish is upgraded with brown rice, barley, and hemp. For a light dinner, serve with buttered green beans and roasted salmon. If there are any leftovers, bulk them up by stirring in tomatoes, cucumbers, and pecans and serve over greens with vinaigrette for a quick salad.

1 tablespoon unsalted butter

½ leek (white and light green parts), thinly sliced

Kosher salt and freshly ground black pepper

½ cup dry white wine (such as sauvignon blanc)

½ cup long-grain brown rice

½ cup pearl barley

1½ cups chicken stock (page 203)

2 tablespoons toasted hemp seeds

½ cup fresh Italian parsley leaves

Melt the butter in a small saucepan over medium heat. Add the leek. Season with salt and pepper. Cook, stirring occasionally, until soft, 3 to 5 minutes. Add the wine and cook, stirring occasionally, until almost evaporated, 4 to 6 minutes. Add the rice and barley and cook, stirring until toasted, 2 to 3 minutes. Add the stock and bring to a boil. Cover the saucepan, reduce the heat to low, and gently simmer until the grains are tender, 35 to 40 minutes. Let sit five minutes. Stir the hemp seeds and parsley into the rice with a fork.

golden polenta cakes with roasted tomatoes and caper berries

MAKES 4 SERVINGS

These supercheesy and rich cakes are creamy on the inside with an impossible-to-resist crispy outside. Serve with roasted pork chops or chicken or over sautéed kale for a vegetarian meal. Caper berries are the slightly larger fruit of a caper bush, while capers are the small immature buds. Look for them in specialty grocery stores or order a jar online. If you can't find caper berries, substitute one tablespoon of capers. The polenta can be made, hardened, and cut into rounds two days in advance; store in an airtight container, in the refrigerator.

1½ cups milk

¾ cup quick cooking polenta

¼ cup toasted hemp seeds

Kosher salt and black pepper

1½ ounces Parmesan, grated

2 tablespoons unsalted butter, cut-up

8 small tomatoes (about 1½ pounds), preferably on the vine

⅓ cup caper berries

2 sprigs fresh oregano

2 garlic cloves, smashed

1 tablespoon red wine vinegar

4 tablespoons olive oil, divided

TIP *Be sure to use a good nonstick sauté pan or well-seasoned cast-iron skillet when frying the cakes: This will ensure that the crisp golden crust doesn't get left behind in the pan.*

Bring the milk and 1½ cups of water to a boil in a medium saucepan. Slowly whisk in the polenta and hemp seeds. Season with salt and pepper. Simmer, whisking constantly, until the polenta is soft and thickened, 6 to 8 minutes. Remove from the heat and stir in the Parmesan and butter. Season with salt and pepper. Transfer the polenta to an 8 x 8-inch baking dish and use a small offset spatula to smooth the surface. Press a piece of plastic wrap directly on the surface of the polenta (this will prevent a hard skin from forming). Chill until firm, 1 hour.

Preheat oven to 425°F.

Drizzle the tomatoes, caper berries, oregano, and garlic with the vinegar and 2 tablespoons of the oil in a 2-quart baking dish. Season with salt and pepper. Roast until the tomatoes are soft, 14 to 16 minutes.

While the tomatoes are roasting, crisp the polenta. Using a 2-inch round cookie cutter, cut the firm polenta into rounds. Heat 1 tablespoon of the oil in a medium nonstick sauté pan over medium heat. Add four of the polenta rounds and cook, without moving, until golden-brown and crisp, 7 to 9 minutes. Flip and cook until golden-brown and crisp on the second side, 7 to 9 minutes. Repeat with the remaining tablespoon oil and polenta rounds.

Serve the polenta cakes with the tomatoes and caper berries, drizzled with any juices in the pan.

roasted mushroom and udon soup with quick pickled vegetables

MAKES 4 SERVINGS

This restorative soup is warm, filling, and the right thing for taking the chill out of a cold winter day. You can use any variety of fresh mushrooms here; as for the other ingredients, look for kombu (large, dark-green, dried edible kelp), bonito flakes (dried, then thinly shaved fish), and dried shiitakes at Asian markets or order them online. Freeze the broth, in an airtight container, for up to three months.

2 small carrots, cut into matchsticks

3 radishes, cut into matchsticks

½ teaspoon finely grated fresh ginger

2 tablespoons unseasoned rice vinegar, plus more for serving

Pinch sugar

2 tablespoons canola oil, divided

Kosher salt

1 cup (1 ounce) dried shiitake mushrooms

1 sheet kombu, rinsed

½ cup (¼ ounce) bonito flakes

½ pound udon noodles

¾ pound mixed mushrooms

2 tablespoons toasted hemp seeds

Fresh cilantro leaves and tender stems

Preheat oven to 425°F.

Combine the carrots, radishes, ginger, vinegar, sugar, and 1 tablespoon of the oil in a bowl. Season with salt.

Place the shiitakes, kombu, and 8 cups of water in a large pot and bring to a boil. Remove from the heat. Discard the kombu. Add the bonito flakes and let sit for 5 minutes. Strain broth through a fine mesh sieve into a pot; discard the solids. Keep the broth warm.

Cook the udon according to the directions on the package. Drain and rinse under cold water to prevent the noodles from sticking together.

While the noodles are cooking, roast the mushrooms. Toss the mushrooms with the remaining tablespoon of oil. Roast, on two large baking sheets, until brown and tender, 8 to 10 minutes.

Divide the noodles between 4 bowls. Top with the broth, hemp seeds, pickled vegetables, and cilantro. Serve with additional rice vinegar.

kale and feta galette with olive oil crust

MAKES 4 SERVINGS

This rustic tart has the flavors of spanakopita—dill, feta, and parsley—but is much easier to prepare than the classic Greek dish. Simply roll out one piece of dough, fill, and fold! Voilà, a simple, yet beautiful meal with little effort. Serve warm or at room temperature. The dough can be made up to three days ahead; store tightly wrapped, in the refrigerator.

1 cup plus 2 tablespoons all-purpose flour, spooned and leveled, plus more for the work surface

¼ cup hemp seeds, finely ground in a spice grinder

Kosher salt and freshly ground black pepper

¼ cup plus 2 tablespoons olive oil, divided

1 medium yellow onion, chopped

1 large bunch kale (about 1½ pounds), stems discarded and leaves torn into small pieces

⅓ cup fresh Italian parsley leaves, chopped

⅓ cup fresh dill, chopped, plus more for garnish

4 ounces creamy feta, crumbled, plus more for garnish

1 large egg yolk

TIP *Ground hemp is sticky, so be sure to break it up and evenly distribute it in the flour when making the dough.*

Preheat oven to 400°F with the oven rack in the lowest position.

Whisk together the flour, hemp seeds, and ½ teaspoon of salt in a bowl. Make a well in the center. Pour ¼ cup of the oil and ⅓ cup of water into the well. Mix until combined. Transfer to an unfloured work surface and knead until the dough comes together, 8 to 10 times. Return to the bowl and let rest for 15 to 20 minutes.

While the dough is resting, make the filling. Heat a large saucepan over medium heat for 30 seconds. Add the remaining 2 tablespoons of oil and heat for 10 seconds. Add the onion. Season with salt and pepper. Cook, stirring occasionally, until the onion is tender, 10 to 12 minutes. Add the kale (if your pot can't hold it all in one go, add a handful, stir until there is room, then add more), and cook, stirring occasionally, until just wilted and still bright green, 6 to 8 minutes. Transfer to a bowl and cool, stirring once to release the heat in the middle, to room temperature. Add the parsley, dill, and feta to the cooled kale and stir to combine. Season with salt and pepper.

Liberally flour a work surface. With a floured rolling pin, roll the dough to a 12- to 13-inch circle. Transfer the dough to a baking sheet.

Place the filling in the center of the dough leaving a two-inch border all around. Working a little bit at a time, bring the border towards the filling, pleating the dough as you work your way around.

TIP *If the kale and feta on the top of the galette start to get dark and dried out when baking, fold up a small piece of foil (the size of the opening) and lay it on top; this will help hold in some of the moisture.*

Combine the egg yolk and 1 teaspoon water in a bowl. Lightly brush the crust with the egg wash (you will have some leftover).

Bake, rotating once, until the crust is golden-brown, 35 to 40 minutes. Let rest 5 minutes.

Serve garnished with feta and dill.

salmon with sautéed cucumber and spicy crème fraîche

MAKES 4 SERVINGS

Warm cucumbers are surprisingly delicious. When quickly sautéed, they take on a more vegetal quality, while retaining their telltale crispiness. Served alongside a tangy crème fraîche, spicy horseradish, and crunchy toasted hemp seed sauce over rich salmon makes for a very elegant, dinner-party-worthy meal.

½ cup crème fraîche

2 tablespoons prepared horseradish, squeezed dry

Kosher salt and freshly ground black pepper

2 tablespoons olive oil, divided

½ English cucumber, halved and sliced

1 tablespoon hemp seeds

4 4-ounce skinless salmon fillets

Chopped fresh chives, for serving

TIP *Avoid stirring the cucumber too much so that it can get golden on one side.*

TIP *Test the doneness of the fish by inserting a paring knife into the center of a fillet. Then, touch the top of the knife to your bottom lip. If it is warm, the fish is done.*

Combine the crème fraîche and horseradish in a bowl. Season with salt and pepper.

Heat a large sauté pan over medium heat for 30 seconds. Add 1 tablespoon of the oil and heat for 10 seconds. Add the cucumber and hemp seeds. Season with salt and pepper. Cook, stirring occasionally, until the cucumber and hemp seeds are golden-brown, 3 to 5 minutes.

Heat the remaining tablespoon of oil in a large nonstick sauté pan over medium-high heat. Season the salmon with salt and pepper. Cook, presentation-side down, until golden-brown, 5 to 6 minutes. Flip and cook until there is just the slightest bit of pink in the middle, about 1 minute.

Serve the fish topped with the spicy crème fraîche, sautéed cucumbers, and chives.

hemp and spinach malfatti

MAKES 4 TO 6 SERVINGS

How can something that translates from Italian meaning "badly made" taste so delicious? Does it refer to the shape? The fact that they are a little shaggy looking? No matter, these soft and creamy dumplings topped with brown butter are pure perfection. Store uncooked dumplings in an airtight container, in the refrigerator, for three days, or in the freezer, for three months. Boil from frozen, adding a minute or two to the cooking time.

Kosher salt

¼ cup plus 2 tablespoons all-purpose flour, plus more for baking sheet

2 10-ounce packages chopped frozen spinach, thawed and squeezed very dry

¼ cup drained whole milk ricotta

1 large egg plus 4 large egg yolks

2 tablespoons toasted hemp seeds

¼ teaspoon freshly grated nutmeg

½ cup (1 stick) unsalted butter, at room temperature, divided

12 large fresh sage leaves

Grated Parmesan, for serving

Bring a medium saucepan of salted water to a rolling simmer. Lightly flour a baking sheet.

Combine the spinach, ricotta, egg and egg yolks, hemp seeds, nutmeg, ¼ cup of the flour, 4 tablespoons of the butter, and 1½ teaspoons of salt in a bowl until the mixture is completely blended.

Form 1 teaspoon of the mixture into a small ball and drop it into the simmering water. If it falls apart, add up to 2 tablespoons of flour to the mixture.

Form the mixture into 12 torpedo-shaped dumplings (about 2 tablespoons each) and place on the prepared baking sheet.

Cook four of the dumplings at a time in the simmering water until they float to the top and are firm, 3 to 4 minutes. Use a spider or slotted spoon to transfer to a plate. Keep warm by covering with a dish towel.

Melt the remaining 4 tablespoons of butter in a medium sauté pan over medium heat. Once the butter is melted, add the sage. Cook, swirling the pan occasionally, until there are golden-brown flecks in the bottom of the pan and the sage is crispy, 3 to 5 minutes. Season with salt.

Serve the dumplings topped with the butter, crispy sage, and Parmesan.

TIP *"Squeezed dry" for the spinach means really squeezed dry: Work hard to get all of the water out of it. If you have a ricer, press the spinach with it to extract the water.*

TIP *To form the dumplings, either roll the mixture between your hands or use two soupspoons.*

steak tacos with hemp tortillas and crispy slaw

MAKES 4 SERVINGS

I lived in Jackson Heights Queens for many years where, on any given day, there were twenty-plus taco trucks lining the main street. In the first year I lived there, I easily ate my weight in tacos. One of the first things that I noticed was that the vendors made every tortilla from scratch and that they roasted whole chiles to give them a smoky flavor (mimicked here in a crunchy roasted poblano and cabbage slaw). It's important to use a very tender steak when making these steak tacos (to keep it from being pulled out of the tortilla in the first bite). Don't be tempted to use a cheaper cut, like a flank or skirt steak (I like a well-marbled New York strip steak). The tortillas can be made one day in advance; store tightly wrapped, in the refrigerator, and steam, as instructed, to reheat.

2 poblano peppers

¼ small head cabbage, shredded

3 scallions, sliced

¾ cup chopped fresh cilantro leaves and tender stems, plus more for serving

¼ cup toasted pepitas

3 tablespoons fresh lime juice

1 small garlic clove, pressed or finely chopped

3 tablespoons olive oil, divided

Kosher salt and freshly ground black pepper

2 cups masa harina

¼ cup toasted hemp seeds

2 well-marbled New York strip steaks (about 1 pound each), 1 inch thick, at room temperature

2 teaspoons ground cumin

Sliced avocado and green hot sauce, for serving

Toast the peppers directly over two burners of a gas stove, set to high, or under a broiler, turning often, until black all over, 8 to 10 minutes. Transfer to a bowl and cover with a piece of foil and allow to cool completely. Once cool, discard the blackened skin, seeds, and stem; coarsely chop.

Combine the chopped peppers, cabbage, scallions, cilantro, pumpkin seeds, lime juice, garlic, and 2 tablespoons of the oil in a bowl. Season with salt and pepper.

Combine the masa, hemp seeds, 1 teaspoon salt, and 1½ cups of water in a second bowl (the mixture should be the consistency of cookie dough). Roll the mixture into 18 balls (about 2 tablespoons each). Transfer the balls to a plate or baking sheet and cover with plastic wrap to keep them from drying out.

Heat a medium nonstick sauté pan over medium heat. Heat a second medium sauté pan over medium-high heat. Fill a pot with 1 inch of water and fit with a steamer basket. Bring to a gentle simmer. Set a clean dishtowel, folded in half, nearby.

Line a tortilla press with plastic wrap. (I've found it works best to use a heavy-duty zip-top bag when pressing the tortillas. Cut it so that it opens on 3 sides and just fits the width of your tortilla press.) Place 1 ball between the plastic and gently press to flatten. Rotate the plastic 180 degrees and press again (this guarantees that the tortilla is an even thickness all the way around). Peel away one side of the plastic. Holding the other side of the plastic in one hand, place the exposed tortilla on your other hand and peel away the plastic. Gently place the tortilla in the pan heated to medium heat. Cook until it is dry and easily releases from the pan, 20 seconds. Flip and cook another 20 seconds. Transfer the tortilla to the pan heated to medium high and cook until golden-brown in spots, 45 seconds per side. Wrap the tortilla in the dishtowel. Repeat with the remaining balls.

Once you have cooked all of the tortillas, fully wrap them in the dishtowel and place in the steamer basket, steam until tender, 10 to 12 minutes.

While the tortillas steam, cook the steak. Heat a large sauté pan over medium heat for 30 seconds. Add the remaining tablespoon of oil and heat for 10 seconds Season the steak with the cumin and salt and pepper. Cook, turning once, until medium-rare, 6 to 8 minutes. Let the steak rest for 5 minutes then thinly slice.

Serve the steak and cabbage in the tortillas topped with the avocado and hot sauce.

TIP *Making the perfect consistency masa dough is not an exact science. If it's very humid out, you may need less water or more masa. If it's dry, the opposite, so be flexible. When pressing the tortillas, if they stick to the plastic, stir in a little more masa. If they crack apart, stir in a little more water.*

plum and hemp crumble

I like to use black plums in this crumble because their bright red interiors make for an incredibly beautiful presentation, but really, any kind will work. The buttery topping is extra nutty from the double dose of pecans and hemp seeds. Give it a try on any single-crust fruit pie—apple and pear with a bit of chopped thyme is a great combo. The port adds a nice depth of flavor, but it's not essential, so feel free to leave it out. Serve warm or at room temperature.

¾ cup all-purpose flour, spooned and leveled

¾ cup pecans, coarsely chopped

½ cup old-fashioned rolled oats

⅓ cup hemp seeds

¾ cup light-brown sugar, divided

¾ teaspoon kosher salt

6 tablespoons unsalted butter, at room temperature, cut up and divided

2 pounds plums, halved and pitted

2 tablespoons port

½ teaspoon finely ground lemon zest

Vanilla ice cream, for serving

Preheat oven to 350°F.

Whisk together the flour, pecans, oats, hemp seeds, ½ cup of the sugar, and ½ teaspoon of the salt in a bowl. Add 4 tablespoons of the butter and use the tips of your fingers to fully incorporate. Squeeze some of the mixture into clumps.

Stir together the plums, port, lemon zest, the remaining ¼ cup of sugar, and the remaining ¼ teaspoon of salt in a bowl. Transfer the plums (making sure they are all cut-side up) and any liquid to a 2-quart baking dish. Top with the remaining 2 tablespoons of butter and the crumble topping. Bake, until the top is golden-brown and the juices are bubbling, 40 to 50 minutes.

Serve warm with a scoop of ice cream.

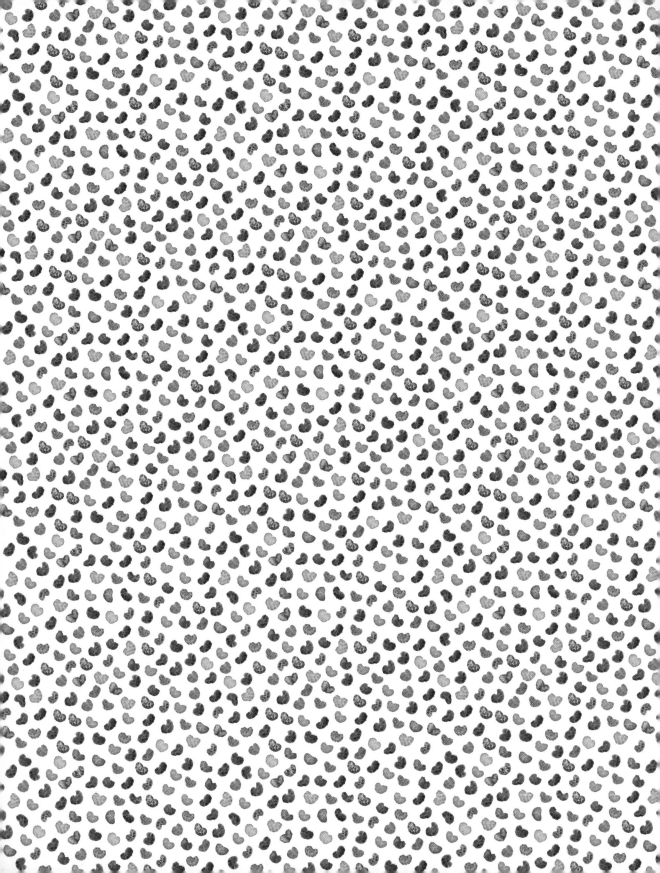

POPPY

The source of poppy seeds, red poppy flowers, has been a symbol of honor throughout history and cultivated for over three thousand years. Poppy seeds come from the same plant that produces opium—*Papaver somniferum*—and are harvested after the plant's latex, which contains the majority of the opiates, has been removed. The latex gets transformed into medical-grade opiates, such as morphine, and the seeds are removed from the dried pods.

Whether coating a bagel or filling a cake, poppy seeds have long had a place at the table. For centuries civilizations have been touting the health benefits of poppy seeds; ancient medical texts promoted them as a cure for infertility and mild insomnia. Poppies contain high amounts of magnesium, phosphorus, calcium, vitamin B, and thiamine. They are incredibly high in fiber and protein—21 and 20 percent, by weight, respectively. The protein in poppy seeds contains all of the major amino acids, suggesting that it is a complete protein.

These diminutive seeds are typically used in small quantities except when baking. But even in the smallest quantity, their crunch adds a lot of texture and their flavor adds a hit of earthiness to any recipe. I love to throw a few tablespoons in pasta dishes with a creamy lemon sauce or as a way to fancy-up southern-style chicken and dumplings. Poppy seed oil has a fruity and intensely earthy flavor. I love a little drizzle over toast topped with ricotta and fresh fruit or over a quick chopped cucumber and onion salad.

TASTE, TEXTURE, APPEARANCE

Poppy seeds are tiny (there are approximately 3,500 per gram), kidney shaped (though you wouldn't notice unless you have a magnifying glass), and, typically, have a blue-black hue. (There are some that are cream, yellow, dark red, and white, but these are not as common.) Their taste is nutty, lightly floral, and earthy. Their texture—incredibly crunchy!

BUYING AND KEEPING

If baking, buy poppy seeds in bulk, either online or in a health-food store that has a bulk section. Otherwise, buy small (spice-sized) jars in the grocery store. Store raw or toasted poppy seeds in a cool, dark place for six months. The oil can be stored in the refrigerator for three months.

TOASTING INSTRUCTIONS

Toasting heightens the flavor of poppy seeds. Toast the seeds in a medium sauté pan over low heat, stirring, until glistening, 2 to 3 minutes, or in a 350°F oven, 8 to 10 minutes. For best results, toast seeds just before using.

poppy milk

MAKES 3 CUPS

Poppy seeds are often a background note, but in this milk their flavor really shines through and is enhanced by the addition of honey. A splash is a perfect pairing with a cup of Earl Grey tea. Store in an airtight container, in the refrigerator, for one week.

1 cup poppy seeds

2 tablespoons honey

Kosher salt

Place the poppy seeds, honey, a pinch of salt, and 3 cups of water in a blender. Blend on high until very smooth, 2 to 3 minutes.

Strain the milk through a nut milk bag or a very fine mesh metal strainer. Chill completely.

poppy, orange, and blueberry smoothie

MAKES 1 SERVING

The color of this smoothie is a little, well, strange, but the flavor is outstanding—vegetal spinach, tangy blueberries, sweet fresh orange juice, and crunchy poppy seeds. Drink it down with a straw or try eating it out of a bowl with a few slices of banana and some chopped nuts or a sprinkle of fresh blueberries, a few grates of lemon zest, and a bit of shaved toasted coconut.

1 cup frozen blueberries

1 cup packed spinach leaves

½ cup fresh orange juice

½ banana

1 tablespoon toasted poppy seeds

Place the blueberries, spinach, orange juice, banana, and poppy seeds in a blender. Blend on high until very smooth, 30 seconds.

> **TIP** *Don't forget to stock the freezer during the height of blueberry season. Spread quarts of fresh berries, in a single layer, on a rimmed baking sheet, and freeze. Once frozen, transfer to a zip-top bag. It will be summer all year long!*

poppy and cashew butter

MAKES 1 CUP

For years I never reached for anything other than a jar of peanut butter because the alternatives were just too darn expensive. Yet once I discovered how much more economical it is to make your own nut butters, my breakfast routine blew wide open. It wasn't just apple slices with a plain old PB smear anymore! While this version has graced many an apple slice, it's also delicious on toast with chopped fresh Ataulfo mango and a sprinkling of cayenne pepper. Store at room temperature, in an airtight container, for two months.

2 cups raw cashews

¼ cup toasted poppy seeds, finely ground in a spice grinder

4 teaspoons canola oil

Kosher salt

Preheat oven to 350°F. Spread the cashews on a small, rimmed baking sheet. Toast until golden-brown and beginning to smell fragrant, 8 to 10 minutes.

Place the cashews, poppy seeds, and oil in a food processor. Process, stopping the food processor and scraping down the bowl as necessary, until the butter is smooth and creamy, 6 to 8 minutes. Season with salt.

TIP *The extra step of grinding the poppy seeds in a spice grinder is necessary because they won't break down in the food processor and will make the butter very crunchy.*

lemon, poppy, and coconut shake

MAKES 1 CUP

With toasted sweetened coconut, zingy lemon zest, and crunchy poppy seeds, this shake makes a perfect dessert topper. Sprinkle a little on lemon pound cake with a small dollop of lightly sweetened whipped cream or coconut sorbet. Store in an airtight container, at room temperature, for one month.

1 cup sweetened shredded coconut

1 strip lemon zest, thinly sliced then chopped

2 teaspoons poppy seeds

Preheat oven to 350°F. Spread the coconut, lemon zest, and poppy seeds on a small, rimmed baking sheet. Toast, stirring frequently, until most of the coconut is golden-brown, 10 to 12 minutes.

sweet and spicy herb sauce

MAKES 1 CUP

A green sauce can take any ho-hum, bland dish and make it spectacular! That's why I like to have a range of sauce recipes in my back pocket when the cooking stars just don't align. This sauce, with spiciness from the red chile and sweetness from the ginger and mirin, is the perfect choice for any Asian-influenced dinner. Try it over roasted fish with bok choy or broccolini. Store in an airtight container, in the refrigerator, for two days.

1 red Serrano chile, chopped

2 packed cups fresh cilantro leaves and tender stems, chopped

⅔ cup packed fresh mint leaves, chopped

½ cup chopped fresh chives

½ cup canola oil

2 teaspoons finely grated fresh ginger

¼ cup fresh lemon juice

4 teaspoons toasted poppy seeds

1 teaspoon mirin

Kosher salt

Combine the chile, cilantro, mint, chives, oil, ginger, lemon juice, and mirin in a bowl. Season with salt.

avocado and grapefruit dip

MAKES 1⅓ CUPS

You might be surprised at the combo of these two ingredients, but creamy avocado paired with tart and juicy grapefruit makes for a refreshing dip. Serve it with tortilla chips as an alternative to guacamole. For the prettiest results, use a pink or red grapefruit. The avocado will start to darken as it sits, so serve the dip as soon as it's made.

1 avocado, chopped

1 grapefruit, peel and pith removed and chopped, juices discarded

1 scallion, sliced

1 tablespoon fresh lime juice

1 teaspoon toasted poppy seeds

Kosher salt and freshly ground black pepper

Combine the avocado, grapefruit, scallion, lime juice, and poppy seeds in a bowl. Season with salt and pepper.

 TIP *When adding the grapefruit, use only the flesh. The juices will make the dip too thin.*

walnut-speckled shredded brussels sprouts

MAKES 4 SERVINGS

Slicing the Brussels sprouts by hand ensures that they are thin, almost ribbony. But if you want to make this side dish quickly, you can use the slicing blade on a food processor. The machine won't slice them as thinly, though, so you will have to increase the cooking time by a minute or two. I always prefer to use fresh herbs versus dried because they have a brighter and, well, fresher taste. But, if you have dried thyme on hand, feel free to substitute one-half teaspoon.

2 tablespoons unsalted butter

2 garlic cloves, chopped

¾ pound Brussels sprouts, stemmed and very thinly sliced

1 tablespoon toasted poppy seeds

1 teaspoon fresh thyme leaves

Kosher salt and freshly ground black pepper

¼ cup roasted walnuts, chopped

4 teaspoons red wine vinegar

1 tablespoon walnut oil

Melt the butter in a large sauté pan over medium-high heat. Add the garlic and cook, stirring, until fragrant, 30 seconds. Add the Brussels sprouts, poppy seeds, and thyme. Season with salt and pepper. Cook, stirring, until the Brussels sprouts are bright green and just tender, 3 to 4 minutes. Stir in the walnuts, vinegar, and oil.

light and refreshing crab salad

MAKES 4 SERVINGS

A crisp green apple provides a nice counterpoint to the salty richness of the crab and the deep taste of the poppies in this perfect-for-summer salad. The sweet flavor of jumbo crabmeat will add a layer of complexity, but its high price may be prohibitive. If so, substitute lump crabmeat: It will work just as well. Serve alongside Bibb lettuce leaves with toast or a few crackers. Because of the soft herbs and apple, this salad is best eaten as soon as it is made.

8 ounces jumbo or lump crabmeat

½ Granny Smith apple, chopped

2 tablespoons fresh chives, chopped

1 tablespoon fresh tarragon leaves, chopped

1 tablespoon olive oil

1 teaspoon lemon zest and 2 teaspoons lemon juice

1 teaspoon toasted poppy seeds

Kosher salt and freshly ground black pepper

Bibb lettuce leaves and toast, for serving

Combine the crab, apple, chives, tarragon, oil, lemon zest and juice, and poppy seeds in a bowl. Season with salt and pepper.

Serve alongside lettuce and toast.

cheddar poppy quick bread

MAKES 1 LOAF

Caramelized onion adds not only moisture but also a sweet, rich flavor to this simple—no mixer required—bread. Balanced with good sharp Cheddar and a bit of salt, it's delicious topped with a smear of butter and a thin slice of prosciutto. Store tightly wrapped, at room temperature, for two days, or slice and freeze for one month.

6 tablespoons unsalted butter, divided, plus more for the pan

1 large sweet onion, chopped

Kosher salt and freshly ground black pepper

3 cups all-purpose flour, spooned and leveled

2 tablespoons toasted poppy seeds

1 tablespoon baking powder

½ teaspoon baking soda

1½ cups buttermilk

1 large egg

2 ounces sharp white Cheddar, grated

Preheat oven to 350°F. Butter a 8½ x 4½-inch loaf pan.

Melt 2 tablespoons of the butter in a medium sauté pan over medium heat. Add the onions. Season with salt and pepper. Cook, stirring occasionally, until golden-brown, 22 to 26 minutes.

Whisk together the flour, poppy seeds, baking powder, baking soda, and 2 teaspoons of salt in a bowl.

Melt the remaining 4 tablespoons of butter in a small saucepan. Whisk together the melted butter, buttermilk, and egg in a bowl. Add the wet ingredients to the dry ingredients and stir to combine. Stir in the onions. Transfer the batter to the prepared loaf pan. Top with the grated Cheddar.

Bake, rotating the pan halfway though, until a toothpick inserted in the center comes out clean, 45 to 55 minutes.

Set the pan on a wire rack and let the bread cool in the pan for 15 minutes. After 15 minutes, use a small offset spatula or butter knife to loosen the bread from the pan. Transfer the bread to the wire rack to cool completely.

> **TIP** *Don't be tempted to turn up the heat when browning the onions. Allow them to go low and slow, instead, so that they get a rich golden-brown color. Toward the end of the cooking time, you will need to stir them frequently because they have less moisture and will want to burn.*

watercress and striped beet salad with pomegranate dressing

MAKES 4 SERVINGS

Pomegranate molasses (available in specialty grocery stores or online) is simply pomegranate juice and sugar that has been reduced to a thick syrup. Its slightly sweet and tangy flavor perfectly balances the crisp and spicy watercress in this salad. I prefer to use watercress, not upland cress, as its firm texture holds up better to the dressing. If you can't find a striped, or Chioggia, beet, use a yellow beet instead. The dressing can be made up to two days in advance.

2 tablespoons olive oil

1 tablespoon pomegranate molasses

1 teaspoon toasted poppy seeds

½ teaspoon honey

Kosher salt and freshly ground black pepper

1 small bunch watercress, thick stems discarded

1 small striped beet, halved and thinly sliced

½ small fennel bulb, thinly sliced

½ cup roasted pistachios, coarsely chopped

Whisk together the oil, pomegranate molasses, poppy seeds, and honey in a bowl. Season with salt and pepper.

Arrange the watercress, beet, fennel, and pistachios on a serving platter. Drizzle with the dressing.

mustard and dill roasted potatoes

Roasted potatoes are incredibly versatile. Serve them hot alongside any protein, cold in a green garden salad, or, as always, at room temperature as part of a BBQ spread. These beauties are a little spicy (from the Dijon), a little tangy (from the vinegar), have a bit of earthiness (from the roasted garlic and poppy seeds), and a fresh green pop from the dill. They're particularly great with baked or grilled chicken thighs. Make one day in advance; store in an airtight container, in the refrigerator. Bring to room temperature and toss with the dill just before serving.

1½ pounds small red potatoes, halved

4 garlic cloves, skin on

2 tablespoons olive oil

Kosher salt and freshly ground black pepper

1 tablespoon poppy seeds

2 tablespoons fresh dill

2 tablespoons Dijon mustard

1 tablespoon red wine vinegar

Preheat oven to 475°F.

Toss together the potatoes, garlic, and oil in a bowl. Season with salt and pepper. Roast on a large, rimmed baking sheet until almost tender, 18 to 20 minutes. Sprinkle on the poppy seeds and continue to roast until the potatoes are tender and the poppy seeds are toasted, 4 to 6 minutes.

Remove the garlic cloves from their skins and roughly chop.

Toss together the potatoes, chopped garlic, dill, mustard, and vinegar. Season with salt and pepper.

> **TIP** *It may seem counterintuitive, but don't toss the potatoes while they are roasting. This will allow the side that is in contact with the pan to get a nice golden and crispy crust. Leaving the garlic cloves in their skins while roasting allows them to get nice and soft without drying out.*

long bean and poppy seed curry

MAKES 4 SERVINGS

For a robust curry, it's important to build the flavors at every step of the pro-cess. Be sure to toast the spices—in this case cumin, coriander, turmeric, poppy, and mustard seeds—and cook the tomatoes until thickened. This will give the dish its signature deep and aromatic flavor. Curry leaves look very similar to bay leaves but have a more herbal fragrance. Like bay, they add a little *je ne sais quoi* that make soups and stews just that much better. Look for them in specialty markets or online.

1 cup basmati rice

1 teaspoon cumin seeds

1 teaspoon coriander seeds

3 tablespoons olive oil

1 yellow onion, chopped

4 garlic cloves, chopped

Kosher salt and freshly ground
    black pepper

1 tablespoon toasted poppy seeds

1 teaspoon turmeric

1 teaspoon yellow mustard seeds

3 large red tomatoes (about
    1½ pounds), chopped

2 small curry leaves

¾ pound long beans, stem end
    trimmed and cut into 2-inch pieces

Fresh cilantro leaves and tender stems
    and plain yogurt, for serving

4 pieces naan, toasted

Cook the rice according to the directions on the package.

Toast the cumin and coriander seeds in a small sauté pan over low heat until fragrant, 1 to 2 minutes. Finely grind in a spice grinder.

Heat a medium saucepan over medium heat for 30 seconds. Add the oil and heat for 10 seconds. Add the onion and garlic. Season with salt and pepper. Cook, stirring occasionally, until the onions are soft, 12 to 14 minutes. Add the ground cumin and coriander, poppy seeds, turmeric, and mustard seeds. Cook, stirring, for 30 seconds.

Add the tomatoes and curry leaves. Season with salt and pepper. Increase the heat to medium high and cook, stirring occasionally, until the tomatoes are broken down and starting to thicken, 12 to 14 minutes. Add the beans. Season with salt and pepper. Cover and cook, stirring occasionally, until the beans are tender, 6 to 8 minutes. Discard the curry leaves.

Serve the curry over the rice, top with the cilantro, yogurt, and the naan alongside.

TIP *A native of Southeast Asia, long beans are similar in flavor to green beans but can grow up to 3 feet long and have a softer texture. Look for them in Asian grocery stores or at farmers' markets. Substitute green beans if you can't track them down.*

chicken soup with poppy seed dumplings

MAKES 4 SERVINGS

My mom and her love of chicken and dumplings inspired this recipe. The broth is flavorful and silky, and the poppy seeds in the dumpling add a deep flavor and nice texture to the whole dish. If you don't have time to make your own stock, use low-sodium chicken broth in its place. You can make the soup up to two days in advance; when ready to serve, bring to a simmer, add the dumplings, and cook as instructed.

2 tablespoons olive oil

4 bone-in, skin-on chicken thighs (about 2 pounds)

Kosher salt and freshly ground black pepper

4 carrots, 1 halved and 3 cut into 1-inch pieces

3 ribs celery, 1 halved and 2 cut into 1-inch pieces

1 small fennel bulb, ½ halved and ½ cored and cut into 1-inch pieces

½ small yellow onion

1 fresh thyme sprig

1½ cups all-purpose flour, spooned and leveled, divided

6 cups chicken stock (page 203)

2 tablespoons toasted poppy seeds

2 teaspoons baking powder

¼ teaspoon baking soda

½ cup buttermilk

1 large egg

1 tablespoon unsalted butter, melted

Heat a large Dutch oven over medium-high heat for 30 seconds. Add the oil and heat for 10 seconds. Season the chicken with salt and pepper. Cook skin-side down, without moving it, until the skin is golden-brown, 4 to 6 minutes. Transfer to a plate.

Add the halved carrot, halved celery, halved fennel, onion, and thyme to the pot. Season with salt and pepper. Cook, stirring occasionally, until the vegetables are brown, 4 to 5 minutes. Whisk in ¼ cup of the flour. Cook, whisking, for 30 seconds. Whisk in the stock. Return the chicken to the pot. Season with salt and pepper. Bring to a boil. Cover, reduce the heat, and simmer, until the chicken is cooked through, 16 to 18 minutes.

Transfer the chicken to a plate. Once cool enough to handle, discard the skin and bones. Shred the meat into large pieces.

Strain the liquid through a fine mesh sieve into a bowl (press to remove as much liquid as possible). Discard the vegetables.

Return the liquid to the pot. Add the chopped carrots, chopped celery, and chopped fennel. Season with salt and pepper. Simmer until the vegetables are starting to soften, 5 to 7 minutes.

While the vegetables are cooking, make the dumplings. Whisk together the remaining 1¼ cups flour, poppy seeds, baking powder, baking soda, and ½ teaspoon salt in a bowl. Whisk together the buttermilk, egg, and butter in a bowl. Add the wet ingredients to the dry ingredients and stir to combine. Drop the mixture (8 mounds) on the simmering liquid. Cover and simmer until the dumplings are cooked through and the vegetables are tender, 10 to 12 minutes.

ham and cabbage oven-roasted hash

MAKES 4 SERVINGS

Hash is often a labor of love, demanding lots of time at the stove frying up different ingredients. This version is every bit as delicious, but for ease it's made in the oven rather than the stovetop—bonus, you can add almost everything at once. It's also less fatty: There are only three tablespoons of oil in the entire recipe. Try it for brunch, served topped with a fried egg, or for a super-easy, hands-off dinner. I use savoy cabbage because I like the soft, thin leaves. If you can't find it, simply use green cabbage and very thinly slice it.

1 pound red fingerling potatoes, halved if large

½ pound ham steak, cut into ¾-inch pieces

1 red onion, cut into 4 wedges, keeping the root intact

1 tablespoon poppy seeds

1 teaspoon coriander seeds, crushed

3 tablespoons olive oil, divided

Kosher salt and freshly ground black pepper

½ small head savoy cabbage, sliced into 1-inch strips

3 tablespoons apple cider vinegar

Sour cream, for serving

Preheat oven to 425°F.

Toss together the potatoes, ham, onion, poppy seeds, coriander seeds, and 2 tablespoons of the oil. Season with salt and pepper. Roast, without tossing, on a large, rimmed baking sheet until the potatoes are almost tender, 14 to 16 minutes.

Toss the cabbage and the remaining tablespoon of oil in a bowl. Season with salt and pepper. Spread on top of the roasting vegetables and continue to roast until the potatoes and cabbage are tender, 6 to 8 minutes.

Toss in the vinegar. Serve with dollops of sour cream.

> **TIP** *It's important not to overcrowd the baking sheet; you want to make sure the ham and potatoes have enough room to brown, not steam. So, if you don't have a large, rimmed baking sheet, bake on 2 smaller baking sheets, rotating them halfway through the first roasting time.*

braised chops with tomatoes and leeks

MAKES 4 SERVINGS

The preparation of these tender chops is another example of complex flavor building. Crisp the bacon, then brown the chops in the bacon fat, next brown the leeks, then add the chopped fresh tomatoes, using their juice to scrape off any stuck-on brown bits in the pan. Serve it all up over creamy polenta or mashed potatoes—essentially, your favorite carb that will soak up the delicious sauce. To guarantee perfectly cooked chops, take the internal temperature with an instant-read thermometer: They are done between 140 and 145°F.

3 slices bacon, chopped

4 bone-in pork chops (about 2½ pounds), 1½ inch thick

1 teaspoon dried oregano

Kosher salt and freshly ground black pepper

2 leeks (white and light green parts), halved or quartered if large, keeping the root intact

1 pound plum tomatoes, chopped

1 tablespoon toasted poppy seeds

½ cup chicken stock (page 203)

Creamy polenta or mashed potatoes, for serving

Cook the bacon in a large, straight-sided sauté pan over medium-high heat, stirring occasionally until brown and crisp, 8 to 10 minutes. Using a slotted spoon, transfer the bacon to a plate; reserve 1 tablespoon fat in the pan.

Season the chops with the oregano and salt and pepper. Cook, in 2 batches, until golden-brown, 3 to 4 minutes per side (they should not be cooked all the way through). Transfer to a plate; reserve the fat in the pan.

Add the leeks cut-side down. Cook, until brown, 1 to 2 minutes. Add the tomatoes and poppy seeds. Cook, stirring occasionally, until the tomatoes are broken down, 6 to 8 minutes. Stir in the stock.

Return the chops to the pan. Simmer until the chops are just cooked through, 8 to 10 minutes.

Slice the chops and serve with the sauce and bacon over creamy polenta or mashed potatoes.

creamy linguine with poppy and prosciutto

MAKES 4 SERVINGS

Poppy seeds and lemon are a classic pair. Combine them with a little heavy cream, pasta, and a few pieces of torn salty prosciutto, and you have a perfectly over-the-top dinner. If you have any leftovers (I highly doubt you will!), to help create more sauce, stir in a few tablespoons of water before reheating in the microwave.

Kosher salt and freshly ground black pepper

2 tablespoons unsalted butter

2 shallots, finely chopped

1 cup heavy cream

1 tablespoon toasted poppy seeds

1 teaspoon finely grated lemon zest

¾ pound linguine

4 ounces prosciutto, torn

TIP *For cream-based pastas, be sure to heat the serving bowl or plates in a low-temp oven (150 or 200°F). This will stop the cream from seizing the second it hits the plate.*

Bring a large pot of salted water to a boil.

While the water comes to a boil, make the sauce. Melt the butter in a large sauté pan over medium heat. Add the shallots. Season with salt and pepper. Cook, stirring occasionally, until tender, 5 to 6 minutes. Add the cream, poppy seeds, and lemon zest. Increase the heat to medium high and simmer until the cream is slightly thickened, 3 to 4 minutes.

Cook the pasta 2 minutes less than the package directions for al dente. Use tongs to transfer the pasta to the sauté pan. Cook the pasta and sauce over medium heat, adding ¼ to ½ cup of the pasta water to the sauté pan, until the pasta is coated and is al dente, 1 to 2 minutes.

Toss in the prosciutto. Season with salt and pepper.

Serve immediately.

TIP *When I'm making pasta that finishes in the sauce, I use tongs to transfer the underdone pasta (two minutes shy of al dente) directly from the boiling water to the sauce. I find it's easier to work over the stove the entire time (no running back and forth between the stove and sink with a big pot of boiling water), and it gives you more leeway for how much pasta water you have available to create the sauce.*

gingery pear poppy seed cake

MAKES 16 SERVINGS

This cake has a double layer of gingery goodness—spicy and hot from the fresh ginger and sweet from the crystallized. Brushing the warm cake with honey not only intensifies the honey flavor but also gives it a beautiful shiny crust. Store at room temperature, wrapped in plastic wrap, for up to three days.

½ cup (1 stick) unsalted butter, plus more for the pan

1 cup all-purpose flour, spooned and leveled, plus more for the pan

1 cup white whole wheat flour, spooned and leveled

¼ cup poppy seeds

1 teaspoon baking powder

1 teaspoon baking soda

½ teaspoon kosher salt

1 cup plain yogurt

⅓ cup plus 1 tablespoon honey, divided

¼ cup granulated sugar

¼ cup packed light-brown sugar

3 tablespoons finely chopped crystallized ginger

1 tablespoon finely grated fresh ginger

3 large eggs

1 teaspoon pure vanilla extract

2 small pears, peeled, cored, and chopped

Preheat oven to 350°F. Butter and flour a 12-cup Bundt pan.

Whisk together the flours, poppy seeds, baking powder, baking soda, and salt in a bowl. Whisk together the yogurt and ⅓ cup of the honey in a bowl.

Beat the butter, sugars, and gingers with an electric mixer on medium-high speed until light and fluffy, 2 to 3 minutes. Add the eggs, one at a time, and beat until fully incorporated. Add the vanilla and beat to combine.

Reduce the mixer speed to low. Gradually beat in one third of the flour mixture. Add one half of the yogurt mixture and beat to combine. Repeat, ending with the remaining third of the flour mixture. Fold in the pears. Transfer the batter to the prepared pan.

Bake, until a toothpick inserted in the center comes out clean, 40 to 50 minutes.

Let the cake cool in the pan for 10 minutes then turn out onto a cooling rack. Microwave the remaining tablespoon of honey in a bowl until thin, about 10 seconds. Brush the cake with the warmed honey.

Eat warm or at room temperature.

lemon and sugar poppy seed crêpes with crème fraîche

MAKES 4 TO 6 SERVINGS

Crêpes are essentially a thin, eggy version of a pancake, and as often happens when making pancakes, the first batch sometimes doesn't turn out so great. But don't worry if your first few are a bust; the recipe is designed to make ten to twelve crêpes, so you have a little wiggle room (and even an ugly crêpe still tastes delicious). The crêpes can be made two days ahead; store tightly wrapped in plastic, in the refrigerator. When you're ready to eat them, drizzle the crêpes with the sugar and lemon, fold into quarters, and reheat in a 350°F oven, in a single layer on a baking sheet, for six to eight minutes.

1½ cups whole milk

1 cup all-purpose flour, spooned and leveled

4 large eggs

3 tablespoons unsalted butter, melted, plus more for the pan

1 tablespoon poppy seeds

¼ teaspoon kosher salt

4 tablespoons plus 1 teaspoon sugar, divided

5 tablespoons fresh lemon juice

Crème fraîche, for serving

Preheat oven to 200°F and place a baking sheet inside.

Place the milk, flour, eggs, butter, poppy seeds, salt, and 2 tablespoons of the sugar in a blender. Blend on high until frothy, 30 seconds to 1 minute. Refrigerate for at least one hour. Pulse the batter once just before using.

Heat a medium nonstick sauté pan over medium-high heat. Dip a pastry brush or balled-up paper towel in butter and grease the bottom of the pan. Pour ¼ cup of the batter into the pan and swirl to spread the batter into a thin even layer.

Cook until the bottom is golden-brown, 2 to 3 minutes. Run a small offset spatula around the edge of the crêpe. Carefully grab the crêpe with your fingers and flip. Cook until cooked through, about 1 minute.

Drizzle each crêpe with 1 teaspoon lemon juice and ½ teaspoon sugar. Fold into quarters. Transfer to the baking sheet. Repeat with the remaining batter, lemon juice, and sugar, buttering the pan between each crêpe.

Serve warm with a dollop of crème fraîche.

blueberry and poppy strudel

MAKES 2 STRUDELS

The dough for these strudels is very similar to brioche—soft, sweet, and buttery—and the vibrant blue filling has a wonderfully deep and complex flavor. The filling can be made up to three days in advance. It will be very stiff when cold and won't spread easily, so be sure to bring it to room temperature and stir it well before using. Store the baked strudel in an airtight container, at room temperature, for up to three days, or freeze for up to one month.

FOR THE DOUGH

4¼ cups all-purpose flour, spooned and leveled, plus more for the work surface

1 teaspoon plus a pinch kosher salt

½ cup unsalted butter, melted, plus more for the bowl

1 cup whole milk, warmed to 100 to 110°F

2 packages active dry yeast (¼ ounce each)

½ cup granulated sugar

3 large eggs

FOR THE FILLING

3 tablespoons unsalted butter

2 cups fresh blueberries

⅓ cup packed light-brown sugar

1 cup poppy seeds, finely ground in a spice grinder

FOR ASSEMBLY

1 large egg yolk

2 tablespoons turbinado sugar

MAKE THE DOUGH

Whisk together the flour and salt in a bowl. Rub the inside of a separate bowl with butter.

Pour the milk into a bowl and sprinkle the yeast. Let sit until the yeast is bubbling, 5 to 7 minutes (if the yeast does not bubble discard the mixture and start again). Whisk in the sugar, eggs, and butter.

Stir the dry ingredients into the wet ingredients, 1 cup at a time, until combined. Turn the dough out onto a floured work surface. Knead until the dough is uniform, about 5 minutes.

Transfer the dough to the buttered bowl and turn to coat with the butter. Cover the bowl with a dishtowel and place it in a warm (but not hot) place. Let the dough rise until doubled in size, 1 to 1½ hours.

MAKE THE FILLING

Melt the butter in a medium saucepan over medium heat. Add the blueberries and sugar. Mash with a potato masher and cook, stirring occasionally, until thickened, 10 to 12 minutes. Stir in the poppy seeds. Cool to room temperature.

POPPY

(continued) ▶

▶ *Blueberry and Poppy Strudel (continued)*

ASSEMBLE THE STRUDELS

Preheat oven to 350°F. Line 2 rimmed baking sheets with parchment paper.

Divide the dough into two equal-sized pieces. Working one piece at a time, roll the dough into a 11 x 14-inch rectangle, on a floured work surface. Spread half of the blueberry mixture on the dough, leaving a 1-inch border on all sides. Roll up the dough lengthwise, keeping it as tight as possible. Transfer to one of the lined baking sheets, seam-side down. Repeat with the remaining dough and blueberry mixture.

Cover the rolls with dishtowels and place them in a warm (but not hot) place. Let the dough rise until slightly puffed, 30 minutes to 1 hour.

Combine the egg yolk and 1 teaspoon water in a bowl. Brush the tops and sides of the rolls with the egg wash (you will have some leftover). Poke the top of each roll five times with the tines of the fork, being sure to go at least three quarters of the way through. (Poking holes in the dough allows steam to escape and helps prevent the dough from cracking. Don't be tempted to poke more holes. Too many weakens the dough and causes large cracks.) Sprinkle with the turbinado sugar, dividing evenly.

Bake, rotating the sheets front to back and top to bottom halfway through, until golden-brown, 25 to 35 minutes.

Eat warm or at room temperature.

refreshing kiwi cooler

MAKES 2 SERVINGS

This drink is a cool refresher for kids or great with a little gin stirred into it for adults. The poppy adds just the tiniest savory note, while a load of fresh mint gives it a bright green color and superfresh flavor. Because the sweetness of kiwis can vary, I have suggested a range of simple syrup amounts.

6 kiwis, peeled

1 cup fresh mint leaves

2 to 3 tablespoons simple syrup

2 tablespoons fresh lime juice

1 tablespoon toasted poppy seeds

Place the kiwis, mint, simple syrup, lime juice, poppy seeds, and 1 cup of ice in a blender. Blend on high until the ice is broken down, 30 seconds.

TIP *To make quick simple syrup, whisk together equal parts warm water and sugar until the sugar is dissolved.*

SUNFLOWER

Sunflower seeds make up the heart of the big, bright yellow flowers you see following the warming rays of the sun in late summer months. The grand golden blossoms have been memorialized throughout history in paintings and poems, and those wanting to add many essential nutrients and vitamins to their diet have long consumed its nutritious seeds. Native to North America, the plant was cultivated by indigenous peoples as early as 3000 BCE. The seeds were ground into flour to make cake and bread, and the expelled oil was used for cooking and hair and skin treatments. After a trip around the world—and intense breeding in Russia to yield larger seeds and a higher oil content—sunflowers have become one of the top five oilseed crops in North America.

When developing these recipes, I was enamored with the heady, nutty fragrance and flavor they added to dishes. They provide balance in a salad of sweet apple and crunchy kohlrabi with a lemony dressing. I love cinnamon sugar toast and couldn't believe that the sugar could actually be improved with the addition of a few chopped sunflower seeds—but it can be!

Sunflower seeds are full of disease-fighting phenolic antioxidants—one-quarter cup provides 82 percent of the vitamin E, 34 percent of the selenium, and 20 percent of the folate you need in a day. Sunflower seeds also contain the essential nutrient choline, which is necessary for healthy cell structure and the synthesis of the neurotransmitter acetylcholine. And they're chock-full of fiber, magnesium, and healthy unsaturated fatty acids. However, because of the high ratio of omega-6 fatty acid in sunflower oil, there is some debate about how healthy the oil is on its own. Sunflower oil tends to be mass produced, is most commonly used for frying and other high-heat cooking, and can be found in many packaged and processed foods. If using, be sure to buy expeller-pressed oil that has been made with organic seeds.

TASTE, TEXTURE, APPEARANCE

The recipes in this chapter all use hulled sunflower seeds. The unhulled seeds are great for snacking (particularly at a baseball game . . . thanks Reggie Jackson!), but the hard outer shells are inedible, thus unsuitable for cooking and baking.

BUYING AND KEEPING

Sunflower seeds are available packaged in most grocery stores, in bulk at health-food stores, and also online. Store unhulled and hulled seeds in the refrigerator for up to six months or in the freezer for up to one year. Store oil in the refrigerator for up to six months.

TOASTING INSTRUCTIONS

Toasting makes hulled sunflower seeds crunchy and increases their yummy nutty flavor. Toast in a medium sauté pan over medium heat, stirring, until light golden-brown and fragrant, 1 to 3 minutes, or in a 350°F oven, stirring once, 8 to 10 minutes. For best results, toast seeds just before using.

sunflower seed milk

MAKES 3 CUPS

A pinch of ground nutmeg gives this milk a subtle savoriness. It's particularly delicious in chai tea or, with a little extra maple syrup stirred in, frozen into a tasty pop. The longer the seeds are soaked, the creamier the milk will be, so plan ahead! Store in an airtight container, in the refrigerator, for up to four days.

1 cup raw sunflower seeds
2 tablespoons maple syrup or agave nectar
Pinch freshly grated nutmeg
Kosher salt

Place the sunflower seeds and 3 cups of water in a bowl. Soak overnight in the refrigerator; drain.

Place the sunflower seeds, maple syrup, nutmeg, a pinch of salt, and 3 cups of water in a blender. Blend on high until very smooth, 2 to 3 minutes.

Strain the milk through a nut milk bag or a very fine mesh metal strainer. Chill completely.

toasted sunflower seed and almond butter

MAKES 1½ CUPS

This recipe went through several iterations. Version one with just toasted sunflower seeds resulted in a butter that was bitter, very sticky, and greenish hued from the oil in the seeds. Round two with only untoasted sunflower seeds lacked depth of flavor. By adding toasted almonds, I achieved a perfect balance of texture and flavor. I knew it was a hit when my friend Alex called to say her seven-year-old, who typically won't eat any nut butters, gobbled it up. Store in an airtight container, in the refrigerator, for two months—although I doubt it will last that long.

2 cups raw almonds
1 cup toasted sunflower seeds
Kosher salt

Preheat oven to 350°F. Spread the almonds on a small, rimmed baking sheet. Toast, until just beginning to smell fragrant, 8 to 10 minutes.

Place the almonds and sunflower seeds in a food processor. Process, stopping the food processor and scraping down the bowl as necessary, until the butter is smooth and creamy, 6 to 8 minutes. Season with salt.

TIP *During the processing, the nuts and seeds get finely chopped, start to look dry, clump up into a big mass, and just when you think it's never going to get creamy—it happens!*

sunflower, cinnamon, and sugar shake

MAKES 1½ CUPS

This is a fun upgrade to classic cinnamon sugar. It has more texture and a deeper flavor because of the seeds. Try it sprinkled on oatmeal with berries or on a banana split with vanilla ice cream and caramel. Store in an airtight container, at room temperature, for up to two months.

½ cup toasted sunflower seeds
¾ teaspoon ground cinnamon
1 tablespoon granulated sugar
Kosher salt

Place the sunflower seeds, cinnamon, sugar, and a pinch of salt in a food processor. Process until finely ground, 10 to 20 seconds.

creamy cherry and sunflower seed smoothie

MAKES 1 SERVING

This ruby-red beauty gets protein and fiber from both the sunflower milk and sunflower seeds and a nice creaminess from the banana. In season, substitute fresh, pitted cherries, plus one-half cup of ice cubes for the recipe's frozen component.

1 cup frozen sweet cherries
½ cup Sunflower Seed Milk (page 149)
½ banana
2 tablespoons toasted sunflower seeds
¼ teaspoon pure vanilla extract

Place the cherries, sunflower milk, banana, sunflower seeds, and vanilla in a blender. Blend on high until very smooth, 30 seconds.

sweet pea and sunflower seed hummus

MAKES 1¾ CUPS

I'm particularly fond of this dip because of its hint of sweetness and bright green color. The avocado makes it extra creamy, and the sunflower seeds give it texture and compliment the flavor of the tahini. Give it a try with the Seeded Apricot and Pecan Crackers on page 101. Make up to one day in advance, but don't stir in the lemon juice until right before serving.

Kosher salt and freshly ground black pepper

1 10-ounce bag frozen peas

¼ cup toasted sunflower seeds

1 garlic clove

½ cup packed fresh cilantro leaves and tender stems

½ avocado

2 tablespoons olive oil, plus more for serving

2 tablespoons fresh lemon juice

1 tablespoon tahini (store-bought or page 14)

½ teaspoon ground cumin

Aleppo pepper

Bring a small saucepan of salted water to a boil. Add the peas and cook until tender, 2 to 3 minutes. Drain and run under cold water to cool completely. Shake to remove as much water as possible.

Place the sunflower seeds and garlic in a food processor and process until finely chopped, 10 to 15 seconds. Add the peas, cilantro, avocado, oil, lemon juice, tahini, and cumin. Process until smooth, 30 seconds to 1 minute. Season with salt and black pepper.

Serve drizzled with oil and sprinkled with Aleppo pepper.

seeded basil pesto

MAKES ¾ CUP

Sunflower seeds add a nuttier taste to this almost-classic basil pesto. Because the basil is blanched (blanching sets the chlorophyll, or green color, in the leaves), the pesto will keep its vibrant green color when stored and also when tossed with hot food. Home from work late and ravenous? Whip up a bowl of pasta with chopped, fresh tomatoes, extra sunflower seeds, a generous dollop of pesto, and a healthy grating of Parm in less than 20 minutes. Store in an airtight container, in the refrigerator, for up to five days.

Kosher salt

2 medium or 1 large bunch basil, leaves removed (about 5 cups)

2 ounces Parmesan, grated

2 tablespoons toasted sunflower seeds

1 garlic clove

⅓ cup olive oil

Bring a medium saucepan of salted water to a boil. Set a bowl of ice water nearby.

Add a large handful of the basil to the water and cook until bright green, about 20 seconds. Use a spider or slotted spoon to transfer to the ice water. Repeat with the remaining basil. Drain the blanched basil and squeeze to remove as much of the water as possible. Coarsely chop.

Place the basil, Parmesan, sunflower seeds, garlic, and ¼ cup of water in a blender. Blend on medium high, stopping the blender and scraping down the jar as necessary, until the mixture is almost smooth, 30 seconds to 1 minute. With the blender running, slowly add the oil through the feed tube. Process until the pesto is smooth, 10 to 20 seconds. Season with salt.

TIP *If you don't have a powerful blender (I use a Vitamix), you may need to add a little more water to get the basil mixture going and a little more oil to get a perfectly smooth emulsion.*

super seedy and nutty energy bars

MAKES 24 BARS

These incredibly filling energy bars—protein from the nuts, fiber from the oats and flax, carbs from the brown sugar and maple—are thick, chewy, and totally addictive. The recipe calls for Toasted Sunflower Seed and Almond Butter, but it's OK to substitute smooth all-natural peanut or almond butter. Use any combination of your favorite nuts; pistachios and peanuts are particularly good. Make 'em grab-'n'-go: Wrap the cut bars individually in plastic wrap and store in the refrigerator, for up to one month.

1½ cups old-fashioned rolled oats

¾ cup raw walnuts, chopped

¾ cup raw pecans, chopped

½ cup raw sunflower seeds

1 cup dried Kalamata figs, chopped

2 tablespoons flax seeds, finely ground in a spice grinder, or ¼ cup flax meal

1 cup cornflakes

Kosher salt

10 tablespoons unsalted butter

¼ cup packed light-brown sugar

¼ cup grade B maple syrup

½ cup Toasted Sunflower Seed and Almond Butter (page 149)

Preheat oven to 350°F. Line an 8 x 8-inch baking dish with parchment paper leaving an overhang on two sides of the pan. (The overhang will help you lift the bars out of the pan.)

Spread the oats, walnuts, pecans, and sunflower seeds on a large, rimmed baking sheet. Toast, stirring once, until just beginning to smell fragrant, 12 to 14 minutes. Cool to room temperature. Place the oat mixture, figs, flax seeds, cornflakes, and 1 teaspoon of salt in a bowl and toss to combine.

Combine the butter, sugar, and maple syrup in a small saucepan. Bring to a boil and cook for 3 minutes.

Add the butter mixture and the Toasted Sunflower Seed and Almond Butter to the dry ingredients and stir until everything is evenly coated. Transfer the mixture to the pan and press very hard on the top to compact (the bottom of a measuring cup works well for this). Refrigerate until fully chilled and firm, at least 12 hours.

Run an offset spatula or butter knife between the parchment paper and pan to help loosen. Transfer to a cutting board and cut into 24 bars (2 x 1 inches each).

sunflower and caraway pretzels

Boiling the pretzels in sweetened baking-soda-laden water sets the pretzels and gives them their distinct dark crust and complex flavor, which nicely complements the the sunflower seeds and caraway. Store the baked pretzels, tightly wrapped, at room temperature, for up to three days, or in the freezer, for up to one month. Toast in a 350°F oven to reheat.

½ recipe pizza dough (page 202)

1 tablespoon caraway seeds

¼ cup baking soda

2 tablespoons light-brown sugar

1 large egg

2 tablespoons olive oil

All-purpose flour, for the work surface

2 tablespoons raw sunflower seeds

Flaky sea salt (such as Maldon)
    or pretzel salt

> **TIP** *If you have a large, wide saucepan, you can boil more than two pretzels at a time. What's important is that the pretzels don't bump into one another.*

Make the pizza dough, whisking the caraway seeds in with the flour mixture before adding the wet ingredients.

Preheat oven to 450°F. Bring the baking soda, sugar, and 12 cups of water to a boil in a large pot. Combine the egg and 1 tablespoon of water in a bowl. Spread the oil on the bottom of two large baking sheets.

Divide the dough into 8 equal-sized pieces (about 2 ounces each). Lightly flour your work surface. Working with one piece of dough at a time, roll the dough, with flat palms, working from the center out, into an 18- to 20-inch rope. Form the rope into a U shape. Fold the ends of the U over twice then down toward the curve; pinch the ends to the curve to attach. Continue flouring the work surface and forming the pretzels. Let the pretzels sit, loosely covered with a dishtowel, for 5 minutes.

Carefully drop 1 to 2 of the pretzels in the boiling water and boil for 30 seconds. Lift the pretzels from the water with a spider or large slotted spoon. Gently tap the spider against the side of the pot to remove as much water as possible. Transfer to the oiled baking sheets. Continue boiling the pretzels.

(continued) ▶

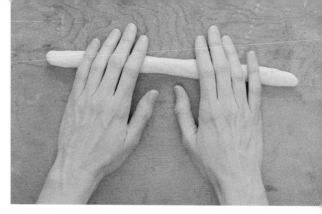

▶ *Sunflower and Caraway Pretzels* (continued)

Lightly brush the boiled pretzels with the egg wash (you will have some leftover) then sprinkle with the sunflower seeds and salt.

Bake, rotating the sheet trays from front to back and top to bottom halfway through, until golden-brown, 12 to 14 minutes.

Serve warm.

> **TIP** *If it's taking you a long time to form the pretzels, keep the already formed ones in the refrigerator while you work so they do not overrise.*

focaccia with sunflower seeds and rosemary

MAKES 16 PIECES

This pillowy focaccia is best eaten as soon as it comes out of the oven. I like rosemary in combination with the sunflower seeds, but go crazy and try it with other savory herbs, like sage or thyme. Be sure to push the sunflower seeds into the dough when making the dimples—it helps them stay attached.

1 recipe pizza dough (page 202)

1 tablespoon finely chopped fresh rosemary

4 tablespoons olive oil, divided

2 tablespoons toasted sunflower seeds

Flaky sea salt (such as Maldon)

Make the pizza dough, whisking the rosemary in with the flour mixture before adding the wet ingredients.

Preheat oven to 450°F.

Spread 3 tablespoons of the oil on the bottom of a jelly-roll pan. Place the dough in the pan and, using your hands, stretch the dough to fit the pan. If the dough springs back while you are stretching it, simply give it a rest for a few minutes; this will give the gluten in the flour time to relax. Once the dough is fully stretched, allow it to rest for 5 minutes.

Sprinkle the sunflower seeds over the dough. Press dimples all over the surface of the dough, using the tips of your fingers, being sure to press some of the seeds down into the dough. Drizzle the top of the dough with the remaining tablespoon of oil and sprinkle with the salt.

Bake until golden-brown, 14 to 16 minutes.

Transfer to a cutting board and cut into 16 pieces. Serve warm.

crispy apple and kohlrabi salad

The combination of nutty seeds, crunchy veggies, and fresh fruit makes this a perfect salad for the start of spring or the waning days of warm weather. Kohlrabi (a knobby bulb sometimes sold with leaves still attached) is that unusual-looking plant you may see hanging around the farmers' market in the spring and fall. A member of the cabbage family, kohlrabi's skin can be green or purple and is edible if the bulb is small. Cut open, the vegetable's flesh ranges in color from pale green to white and is immensely crispy and a little sweet.

1 red-skinned apple, cut into matchsticks

2 small purple kohlrabi, cut into matchsticks

¼ cup fresh tarragon leaves

3 tablespoons toasted sunflower seeds

3 strips lemon zest, thinly sliced lengthwise

1 tablespoon olive oil

1 tablespoon fresh lemon juice

Flaky sea salt (such as Maldon) and freshly ground black pepper

Arrange the apple, kohlrabi, tarragon, sunflower seeds, and lemon zest on a serving platter. Drizzle with the oil and lemon juice. Season with salt and pepper.

 TIP *Use a vegetable peeler to remove the lemon zest. If any of the bitter white pith is attached, remove it with a sharp paring knife, then cut it into long pretty strips.*

harissa wheat berry salad

MAKES 4 SERVINGS

Wax beans are simply a variety of green beans with a different name and color—and they are not at all waxy. They add a nice pop of yellow color to the salad, but if you can't find them, simply use the green standby. The cooking time for the wheat berries will result in grains that are al dente. If you prefer them softer, simply keep cooking them! This salad gets a real kick from the *harissa*. If making your own is not in the cards you can find store-bought varieties, but if I do say so, they don't hold a candle to homemade. Make this salad up to twelve hours ahead, but don't add the dressing, nor season with salt and pepper, until just before serving.

Kosher salt and freshly ground black pepper

1 cup wheat berries

2 Persian cucumbers, chopped

4 ounces wax beans, thinly sliced

½ cup toasted sunflower seeds

⅓ cup fresh mint leaves, torn if the leaves are large

¼ small red onion, thinly sliced

2 tablespoons harissa (page 206)

2 tablespoons olive oil

1 tablespoon sherry vinegar

Bring a small saucepan of salted water to a boil. Add the wheat berries and simmer until al dente, 45 to 50 minutes. Drain and run under cold water to cool completely. Shake to remove as much water as possible. Spread the wheat berries on a small baking sheet or plate and refrigerate, stirring once, until the grains are completely dry, 30 minutes.

Combine the wheat berries, cucumber, beans, sunflower seeds, mint, onion, *harissa*, oil, and vinegar in a bowl. Season with salt and pepper.

smoked curry chicken salad

MAKES 4 SERVINGS

This sweet and smoky salad is a perfect summertime staple. My preferred wood for smoke is apple or lilac because they provide a mild, slightly sweet smoky flavor. (If you are unable to smoke the chicken simply roast it in the oven.) See page 9 for instructions on how to set up the grill. Store in an airtight container, in the refrigerator, for up to two days.

1 whole chicken, about 4 pounds

Kosher salt and freshly ground black pepper

½ cup mayonnaise

2 ribs celery, chopped

1 shallot, finely chopped

⅓ cup golden raisins

¼ cup toasted sunflower seeds

2 tablespoons fresh lemon juice

1½ teaspoons curry powder

Heat grill to medium and set up for indirect heat grilling. Soak a small piece of apple wood or lilac wood in water for 15 minutes.

Season the chicken with salt and pepper. Tie the legs together with twine and tuck the wings under the body.

Place the soaked wood directly on the coals if using a charcoal grill, in a smoker box, placed over the heat source, if using a gas grill. Place the chicken on the unheated side of the grill. Cover (leaving the grill vent open directly above the chicken) and grill, breast-side up and rotating the chicken 90 degrees once, until the internal temperature reaches 165°F, 1 hour to 1 hour 15 minutes. Cool completely.

Discard the chicken skin and remove as much meat from the chicken as possible (you should have between 4 and 5 cups). Shred the chicken into large pieces.

Combine the chicken, mayonnaise, celery, shallot, raisins, sunflower seeds, lemon juice, and curry powder in a bowl. Season with salt and pepper.

TIP *Don't throw away the chicken carcass! Simmer it in a pot of water with an onion and a few carrots for one of the best smoky chicken stocks you will ever have!*

SUNFLOWER

mushroom tamales with a tomatillo sunflower seed sauce

This best-for-the-weekend project is a little time consuming but well worth the effort for a light, fluffy, and delicious tamale. The deep flavor of the mushrooms perfectly balances the tangy, bright, and nutty flavor of the sauce. If possible, buy masa harina ground specifically for making tamales: Its coarser grind will ensure a lighter end result. When buying tomatillos, peel back a little of the paper to make sure that the fruit is firm and plump. The mushroom filling and tamale batter can be made two days ahead. (Before using the batter, beat it for a minute or so to loosen.) Serve as a meal with rice and beans, as an appetizer, or as part of a buffet.

14 large dried cornhusks

FOR THE TAMALE DOUGH

1¾ cups masa harina

⅔ cup nonhydrogenated vegetable shortening or lard

1 teaspoon baking powder

Kosher salt

¾ cup vegetable stock (page 204)

FOR THE FILLING

½ ounce dry porcini mushrooms

2 tablespoons olive oil

¼ small yellow onion, finely chopped

2 garlic cloves, finely chopped

Kosher salt

8 ounces cremini mushrooms, finely chopped

½ poblano pepper, seeded and finely chopped

FOR THE SAUCE

1 tablespoon olive oil

¾ pound tomatillos, papery skins discarded, chopped

2 garlic cloves, chopped

1 jalapeño pepper, chopped

Kosher salt and freshly ground black pepper

1 cup fresh cilantro leaves and tender stems

2 scallions, sliced

2 tablespoons toasted sunflower seeds

2 tablespoons fresh lime juice

1 tablespoon green Tabasco sauce

TIP *Look for masa harina and dried cornhusks in Latin markets or order online.*

(continued) ▶

Soak the cornhusks in water for at least 1 hour.

MAKE THE TAMALE DOUGH

Combine the masa and 1 cup of water in a bowl until everything just holds together. If there is still dry masa at the bottom of the bowl, add up to 2 additional tablespoons of water. Beat the shortening, baking powder, and 1 teaspoon salt in an electric mixer until light and fluffy, 1 to 2 minutes. Add half of the masa mixture and half of the stock and beat until combined. Add the remaining masa mixture and stock and beat until light and fluffy, 2 to 3 minutes. To test that the dough is properly beaten, scoop a little into a small glass of water. It should float; if it doesn't, beat a minute longer. Refrigerate the dough until chilled completely, 45 minutes to 1 hour.

MAKE THE FILLING

Soak the porcini in ½ cup warm water until soft, 20 to 30 minutes. Lift the mushrooms from the soaking liquid and finely chop. Strain the soaking liquid through a fine mesh sieve to remove any grit; reserve the liquid.

Heat a large sauté pan over medium heat for 30 seconds. Add the oil and heat for 10 seconds. Add the onion and garlic. Season with salt. Cook, stirring occasionally, until the onion is beginning to soften, 3 to 4 minutes. Add the cremini mushrooms and poblano. Season with salt. Cook, stirring occasionally, until the mushrooms have released their liquid and are golden-brown, 8 to 10 minutes. Add the chopped porcini mushrooms and soaking liquid. Cook until the liquid is absorbed, 3 to 4 minutes. Season with salt. Cool completely.

ASSEMBLE THE TAMALES

Fit a large stockpot with a steamer basket and add just enough water so that it comes just to the bottom of the basket. Bring to a simmer.

Drain the soaked cornhusks and pat dry with paper towels. Reserve the 12 largest and most intact (those without any cracks or tears). If your cornhusks have stiff, thick bottoms, cut off the thick part with kitchen shears before assembling the tamales. The stiffness will make folding hard. Tear the remaining 2 into long ½-inch-wide strips—these strips will be used to tie the rolled tamales so they hold together while they steam.

Beat the chilled tamale dough until light and fluffy, 30 seconds to 1 minute.

Place a little of the tamale dough (about ¼ cup) in the middle of one of the cornhusks, being sure to leave a 1½-inch border on the bottom. Flatten the dough into a 4- to 5-inch square, with a small offset spatula. Place a little of the mushroom filling (about a heaping tablespoon), lengthwise, down the center of the dough, leaving a small border on the top and bottom. Working from the sides, use the cornhusk to help you bring the dough together and encase the filling (don't worry if a few bits of mushroom are left exposed). Once the filling is encased, fold up the bottom of the cornhusk, fold in the sides, and then fold down the top. Use a strip of cornhusk to tie the package together. If the thin strips of torn cornhusks are not long enough to go around the formed tamales, simply tie two strips together to create a longer length. Repeat with the remaining cornhusks, dough, and filling.

(continued) ▶

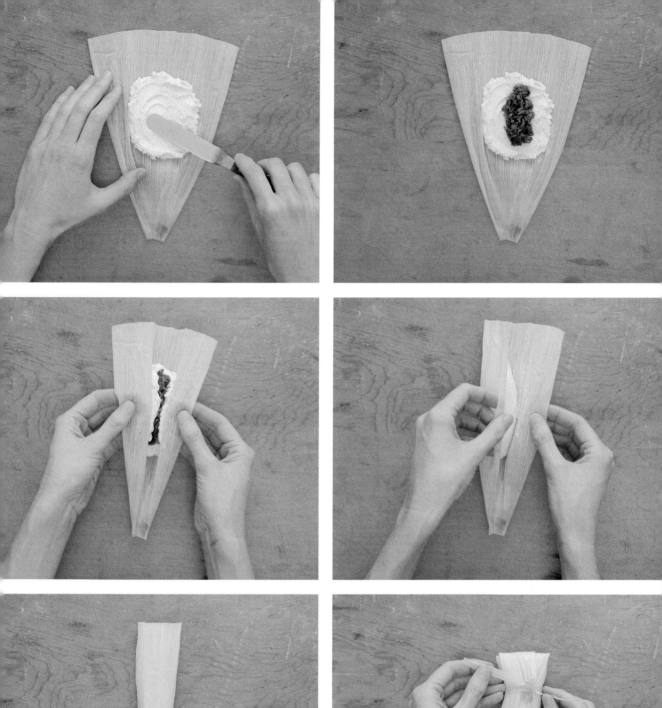

Set the tamales upright in the steamer basket and steam until the tamales no longer stick to the sides of the cornhusks, 1 hour 10 minutes to 1 hour 15 minutes. While the tamales are steaming, set your timer to go off every 20 to 30 minutes to check the water level in the pot. If the pot runs out of water, the bottom will scorch and give the tamales a very unpleasant burnt taste.

MAKE THE SAUCE

Heat a medium sauté pan over medium heat for 30 seconds. Add the oil and heat for 10 seconds. Add the tomatillos, garlic, and jalapeño. Season with salt and pepper. Cook, stirring occasionally, until the tomatillos are beginning to get soft, 12 to 14 minutes. Place the tomatillo mixture, cilantro, scallion, sunflower seeds, lime juice, and Tabasco in a blender. Blend on high until smooth, 30 seconds to 1 minute. Season with salt and pepper.

Serve the tamales with the sauce.

thai style stir-fry with ground pork and swiss chard

MAKES 4 SERVINGS

This is a riff on the Thai dish *larb*. In the classic iteration, ground pork is sautéed then tossed with the aromatics and sauce and served with lettuce leaves. In this version, I cook the scallion, garlic, and ginger to soften their flavors a bit then toss in Swiss chard at the end. Serve over rice and voilà! A quick dinner that has deep complex flavors. Thai bird chiles (look for them in Asian markets) can be very spicy, so if you are spice averse, use only half or maybe even only a quarter. If you can't get your hand on a Thai bird, substitute a jalapeño.

1 cup short-grain white rice

2 tablespoons fish sauce

2 tablespoons unseasoned rice vinegar

1 teaspoon light-brown sugar

3 tablespoons canola oil

1 medium bunch Swiss chard, stems thinly sliced and leaves torn

3 scallions, chopped

3 garlic cloves, chopped

1 tablespoon finely chopped fresh ginger

Kosher salt and freshly ground black pepper

1 pound ground pork

½ to 1 Thai bird chile, seeded and chopped

¼ cup toasted sunflower seeds

Thai basil, Sriracha, and lime wedges, for serving

Cook the rice according to the directions on the package.

Combine the fish sauce, vinegar, and brown sugar in a bowl.

Heat a large sauté pan over medium-high heat for 30 seconds. Add the oil and heat for 10 seconds. Add the chard stems, scallions, garlic, and ginger. Season with salt and pepper. Cook, stirring, until the chard stems are tender, 3 to 5 minutes. Add the pork and chile. Season with salt and pepper. Cook, stirring occasionally, until the pork is cooked through, 4 to 6 minutes. Add the chard leaves (if your sauté pan can't hold them all in one go, add a handful, stir until just wilted, then add more), sunflower seeds, and fish sauce mixture. Cook, stirring, until the chard leaves are just wilted, 2 to 3 minutes.

Serve the pork and chard over the rice topped with the Thai basil and Sriracha and the lime wedges on the side.

stuffed collard greens
with tart tomato sauce

This all-in-one meal is filling and satisfying. It has a hint of smoke from the bacon, sweet aromatics from the paprika, and an unexpected crunch from the sunflower seeds. To crush the tomatoes, either break them up with your hands or mash them in the pot with a potato masher. Being from the South, I like to cook my own black-eyed peas, but it's OK to use canned or frozen. The collards can be blanched, rice mixture cooked, and sauce made up to two days ahead. Assemble and bake just before serving.

Kosher salt and black pepper

12 large collard green leaves, thick stems discarded

2 tablespoons olive oil

2 garlic cloves, chopped

½ teaspoon red pepper flakes

1 28-ounce can whole peeled tomatoes, crushed into small pieces

1 teaspoon cider vinegar

5 slices bacon, chopped

1 rib celery, chopped

1 small yellow onion, chopped

1 green bell pepper, seeded and chopped

2 tablespoons fresh oregano leaves, chopped

½ teaspoon sweet paprika

¾ cup long-grain white rice

¼ cup toasted sunflower seeds

1 cup cooked black-eyed peas

Bring the large pot of salted water to a boil. Boil the collards, 1 to 2 at a time, until bright green and tender, 30 to 40 seconds. Use a spider or slotted spoon to transfer to a plate. Pat dry with paper towels.

Heat a medium saucepan over medium-high heat for 30 seconds. Add the oil and heat for 10 seconds. Add the garlic and red pepper flakes and cook, stirring, until fragrant, 20 to 30 seconds. Add the tomatoes. Season with salt. Simmer, stirring occasionally, until thickened, 20 to 22 minutes. Stir in the vinegar. Pour into a 2-quart baking dish.

While the sauce is simmering, make the rice. Cook the bacon in a small saucepan over medium heat, stirring occasionally, until brown, 10 to 12 minutes. Using a slotted spoon, transfer the bacon to a small plate, reserving the fat in the saucepan. Add the celery, onion, pepper, and oregano to the saucepan. Season with salt and pepper. Cook, stirring occasionally, until the vegetables are tender, 6 to 8 minutes. Add the paprika and cook, stirring, until darkened, 20 to 30 seconds. Add the rice and 1 cup of water and bring to a boil. Cover the saucepan, reduce the heat to low, and gently simmer until the rice is tender, 14 to 16 minutes. Let sit 5 minutes. Stir the sunflower seeds, peas, and cooked bacon with a fork.

Place a little of the rice (about ⅓ cup) in the middle of one of the collards. Fold the sides over the filling, then roll, lengthwise, to completely enclose. Place, seam-side down, on the tomato sauce. Repeat with the remaining collards and rice.

Cover the baking dish with foil and bake until the sauce is bubbling, 25 to 35 minutes.

red snapper over crisp chickpeas with sunflower seed chermoula

MAKES 4 SERVINGS

Crispy chickpeas are a thing of wonder, creamy on the inside and crispy, like a french fry, on the outside. The sauce for this dish is one of my favorites— tangy and spicy with a bit of crunch from the sunflower seeds. Bring it all together with a perfectly seared piece of fish.

1 cup packed cilantro leaves and tender stems, chopped

1 garlic clove, finely chopped or pressed

2 tablespoons white wine vinegar

2 tablespoons toasted sunflower seeds, chopped

1 teaspoon sweet paprika

¾ teaspoon ground cumin

½ to 1 teaspoon red pepper flakes

8 tablespoons olive oil, divided

Kosher salt and freshly ground black pepper

1¼ cups cooked chickpeas

1 bunch flat-leaf spinach, stems discarded

4 4 to 6 ounce skin-on red snapper fillets

Combine the cilantro, garlic, vinegar, sunflower seeds, paprika, cumin, red pepper flakes, and 5 tablespoons of the oil in a bowl. Season with salt and black pepper.

Heat 2 tablespoons of the oil in a medium nonstick skillet over medium-high heat. Add the chickpeas and cook, stirring occasionally, until crispy, 6 to 8 minutes. Add the spinach (if your sauté pan can't hold them all in one go, add a handful, stir until just wilted, then add more) and cook until just wilted and still bright green, 1 to 2 minutes. Season with salt and black pepper.

Heat the remaining tablespoon of oil in a large nonstick skillet over medium-high heat. Pat the snapper dry with paper towels. Season with salt and black pepper. Cook, skin-side down, pressing the fish down with a spatula to guarantee that all of the skin is in contact with the pan, until the skin is golden-brown and crispy, 3 to 4 minutes. Carefully flip the fish and cook until cooked through, 1 to 2 minutes.

Serve the fish and vegetables drizzled with the *chermoula*.

> **TIP** *I recently discovered the hands-down best way to cook dried chickpeas—use a pressure cooker! No longer are these the scary "Is it going to explode and burn the house down?" contraptions of the 1950s. Modern-day pressure cookers are safe and incredibly time saving. Soak dried chickpeas overnight, drain, and cook (usually no more than 15 minutes). The chickpeas are perfectly intact and creamy every time.*

grilled steak with beets and bitter greens

This is a perfect summer dinner salad because it doesn't require turning on the oven, heating up the kitchen, and driving the AC bill up. The steak and beets are grilled, and then tossed with a sweet and crunchy dressing that helps tame the bitterness of the greens. Gild the lily—whisk any steak juices that accumulate from resting into the dressing.

3 tablespoons white wine vinegar

1 tablespoon honey

2 tablespoons toasted sunflower seeds, coarsely chopped

4 tablespoons olive oil, divided

Kosher salt and freshly ground black pepper

2 medium yellow beets (about ½ pound), peeled and each cut into 4 wedges

1 well-marbled New York strip steak (about 1 pound), 1 inch thick, at room temperature

1 head radicchio, torn into bite-sized pieces

½ cup cornichons, halved lengthwise

½ cup fresh Italian parsley leaves, torn if large

Heat grill to medium-high heat and set up for both indirect and direct grilling (see page 9 for tips).

Whisk together the vinegar, honey, sunflower seeds, and 3 tablespoons of the oil in a bowl. Season with salt and pepper.

Toss the beets with the remaining tablespoon of oil. Season with salt and pepper. Grill the beets over indirect heat, covered and turning occasionally, until tender, 18 to 20 minutes.

Season the steak with salt and pepper. Grill over direct heat, uncovered, turning occasionally and moving away from any grill flare-ups, until medium-rare, 6 to 8 minutes. Let the steak rest for 5 minutes then thinly slice.

Toss together the radicchio, cornichons, parsley, grilled beets, sliced steak, and dressing. Season with salt and pepper.

> TIP *Be systematic when making this dinner: start heating the grill, prep the dressing and salad, then get grilling. No access to a grill? Pan-sear the steak and roast the beets in the oven.*

chocolate cupcakes
with seed butter ganache

Reminiscent of devil's food cake, these supermoist cupcakes are topped with a chocolate ganache that has a little added bonus—Toasted Sunflower Seed and Almond Butter. Trust me, it won't take long for all twenty-four to be gobbled up. For a kids' party, decorate them with a sprinkle of candy-coated sunflower seeds. If you can't find Dutch-processed cocoa powder, substitute the natural variety, and don't worry if you don't have two cupcake tins; simply cook one batch, reline the pan, and bake the second batch. The cupcakes can be made one day in advance; store in an airtight container, at room temperature.

1¾ cups all-purpose flour, spooned and leveled

¼ cup white whole wheat flour, spooned and leveled

1½ cups granulated sugar

¾ cup Dutch-processed cocoa powder

½ cup packed light-brown sugar

1 teaspoon baking soda

1 teaspoon kosher salt

1 cup (2 sticks) unsalted butter

2 large eggs

1 teaspoon pure vanilla extract

½ cup plain Greek yogurt

1 cup heavy cream

8 ounces semisweet chocolate, chopped

⅔ cup Toasted Sunflower Seed and Almond Butter (page 149)

Preheat oven to 350°F. Line two 12-cup standard muffin tins with liners.

Whisk together the flours, granulated sugar, cocoa, light-brown sugar, baking soda, and salt in a bowl. Combine the butter and 1 cup of water in a small saucepan. Simmer until the butter is melted.

Whisk the butter mixture into the dry ingredients until combined. Whisk in the eggs, one at a time, being sure the first is fully incorporated before adding the second. Whisk in the vanilla and yogurt until combined. Divide the batter between the lined cups (about ⅓ cup each). Bake, rotating the tins front to back and top to bottom halfway, until a toothpick inserted in the center comes out clean, 16 to 18 minutes.

Set the tins on a wire rack and let the cupcakes cool in the pan for 15 minutes. Then transfer to the wire rack to cool completely.

While the cupcakes cool, make the ganache. Bring the cream to a boil in a small saucepan. Remove from the heat and add the chocolate (give the pan a few shakes to make sure that all of the chocolate is covered.) Let sit for 5 minutes then whisk until smooth. Whisk in the Toasted Sunflower Seed and Almond Butter until smooth. Frost the cupcakes with ganache.

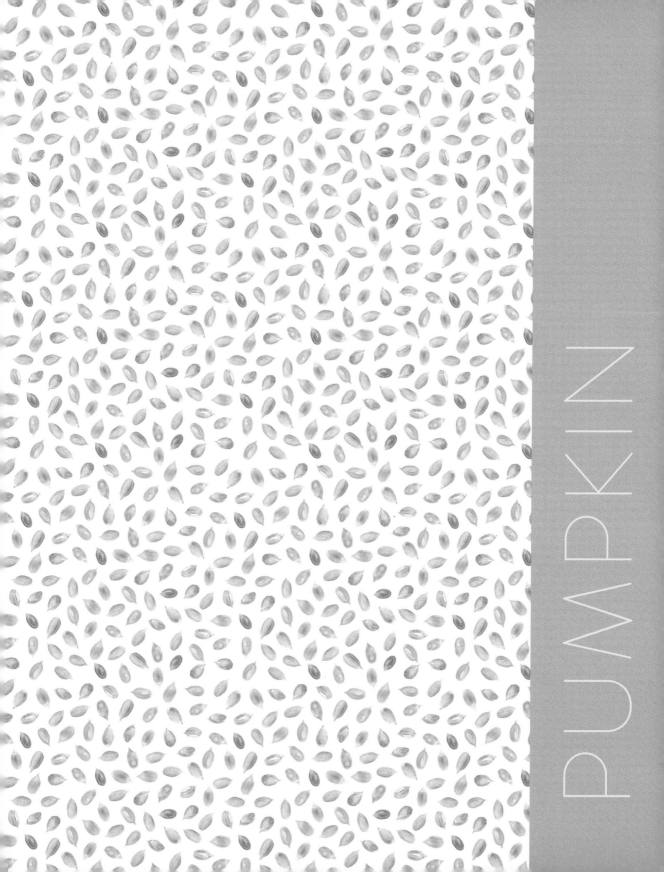

PUMPKIN

While the name *pumpkin* originated from the Greek—*pepon* meaning "large melon"—the vegetable is purported to have first been cultivated in Central America. Seeds from nearly nine thousand years ago have been discovered in Mexico. The fruit (yes, it's a fruit not a vegetable!) then began its journey to the New World, Europe, and even farther afield. As I mentioned, I love to garden, and hands-off pumpkins and winter squash are one of my favorite things to grow. Early in the summer, drop a few seeds or put a few starter plants in the far reaches of the garden, and then go about your summer business—swimming, canoeing, late nights by the fire pit. Come back many weeks later, and you'll find plants laden with dense, colorful, and funny-shaped squash. Stash the squash in a cool, dark spot, and they will keep for months. While roasting the seeds from your pumpkin (or any winter squash for that matter) is a must come October 31, using them in recipes can be a bit of a disaster. The seed coats never fully soften and leave unwanted hard bits. Thus, when developing the recipes for this chapter, I only used hulled seeds, aka pepitas. I love the way they add a squash-like flavor to dishes, and their beautiful green color is appealing to the eye.

Pumpkin seeds are 50 percent oil and contain a whopping 35 percent protein but have no starch. They also contain high levels of omega-3 and omega-6 fatty acids, magnesium (a quarter cup has almost half the daily recommended amount), and fiber. Pumpkin seed oil has an amazingly nutty flavor. Depending on whether the oil has been made from toasted or untoasted seeds, it can range in color from brown (toasted) to bright green (untoasted).

TASTE, TEXTURE, APPEARANCE

There are two types of pumpkin seeds available in the market, unhulled and hulled. Unhulled seeds (the ones coated in goo on the inside of your jack-o'-lantern) still contain their hard, white-colored seed coat. Hulled seeds are known as pepitas. Pepitas have a green hue, a light yet crunchy texture, and a squash-like flavor.

BUYING AND KEEPING

Pepitas are available packaged in most grocery stores, in bulk at health-food stores, and also online. Store in an airtight container, in the refrigerator, for up to two months or in the freezer for up to six months. Store pumpkin seed oil in the refrigerator for up to six months.

TOASTING INSTRUCTIONS

Toast in a medium skillet over medium heat, stirring occasionally, until puffed and golden-brown, 4 to 6 minutes, or in a 350°F oven, until fragrant and starting to pop, 12 to 14 minutes. For best results, toast hulled seeds just before using.

maple pumpkin seed milk

MAKES 3 CUPS

This milk has the nuttiest flavor of any in this book. It's great with the Tropical Fruit Muesli (page 19) and the Toasted Cashew, Coconut, and Molasses Granola (page 99) because all of the flavors really build on each other.

1 cup hulled pumpkin seeds

2 tablespoons pure maple syrup

Kosher salt

Place the pumpkin seeds and 3 cups of water in a bowl. Soak overnight in the refrigerator; drain.

Place the pumpkin seeds, maple, a pinch of salt, and 3 cups of water in a blender. Blend on high until very smooth, 2 to 3 minutes.

Strain the milk through a nut milk bag or a very fine mesh metal strainer. Chill completely.

spinach apricot smoothie

MAKES 1 SERVING

You may think of spinach and fruit as a more salady type of combination, but the tangy apricot juice perfectly balances the green flavors of the spinach and pumpkin seeds in this morning pick-me-up. If you can only find large bottles of apricot juice and don't want to drink it on its own, freeze any leftover in ice-cube trays. Once it is frozen, transfer it to a zip-top bag. Use a few extra frozen cubes of juice in place of the ice.

2 cups baby spinach

1 cup apricot juice

2 tablespoons hulled pumpkin seeds

Place the spinach, apricot juice, pumpkin seeds, and ½ cup of ice in a blender. Blend on high until smooth, 30 seconds.

cinnamon pumpkin seed butter

MAKES 1½ CUPS

Cinnamon is a common spice used to flavor roasted pumpkin seeds because its deep warm flavor elevates the seed's complex nuttiness. Try this spread on raisin toast for a classic breakfast combo or sandwiched between chocolate wafer cookies for a quick snack. Store in an airtight container, in the refrigerator, for two months.

1 cup almonds

2 cups toasted hulled pumpkin seeds

1 teaspoon ground cinnamon

Kosher salt

Preheat oven to 350°F. Spread the almonds on a small, rimmed baking sheet. Toast until just beginning to smell fragrant, 8 to 10 minutes.

Place the almonds, pumpkin seeds, and cinnamon in a food processor. Process, stopping the food processor and scraping down the bowl as necessary, until the butter is smooth and creamy, 6 to 8 minutes. Season with salt.

pumpkin seed, dill, and lime sauce

MAKES 1 CUP

Bright and herbaceous, this zippy little sauce is great over roasted chicken thighs, pan-seared steak, or the Arctic Char and Broccolini (page 195). Because of the delicate fresh herbs, it's best eaten the day it is made.

1 packed cup fresh cilantro leaves and tender stems, chopped

½ cup fresh dill, chopped

⅓ cup olive oil

¼ cup toasted hulled pumpkin seeds, chopped

1 small garlic clove, chopped

½ teaspoon finely grated lime zest and 1 tablespoon fresh lime juice

Kosher salt and black pepper

Combine the cilantro, dill, oil, pumpkin seeds, garlic, and lime zest and juice in a bowl. Season with salt and pepper.

spiced pumpkin seed shake

MAKES ⅓ CUP

Extra crunchy from the pumpkin seeds and full of flavor from the warming spices, this shake is great on Sausage and Squash Stew (page 192) or sprinkled on hummus or white bean dip. Store in an airtight container, at room temperature, for up to one month.

¼ cup toasted hulled pumpkin seeds, finely chopped

2 teaspoons dried oregano

1 teaspoon cumin seeds, coarsely ground in a spice grinder

½ teaspoon sweet paprika

½ teaspoon smoked paprika

Kosher salt and freshly ground black pepper

Combine the pumpkin seeds, oregano, cumin seeds, and paprikas in a bowl. Season with salt and pepper.

pumpkin seed and parsley dip

MAKES 1 CUP

This rich, creamy, and brightly flavored version of a traditional Mexican dip is guaranteed to be a great addition next to the chip bowl on your dinner party appetizer spread. Typically made with a mix of fresh herbs, this version keeps it simple and only calls for parsley. Make up to one day ahead; store in an airtight container, in the refrigerator. Give it a quick taste before serving. If it's lost its telltale zip, stir in a little vinegar and salt to perk it up.

⅓ cup plus 1 tablespoon olive oil, divided

2 scallions, chopped (white and dark green parts separated)

1 garlic clove, chopped

Kosher salt

2 teaspoons red pepper flakes

½ cup toasted hulled pumpkin seeds

1 packed cup fresh Italian parsley leaves

3 tablespoons red wine vinegar

Heat a small saucepan over medium heat for 30 seconds. Add 1 tablespoon of the oil and heat for 10 seconds. Add the scallion whites and garlic. Season with salt. Cook, stirring occasionally, until the scallions are tender, 2 to 3 minutes. Add the red pepper flakes. Cook, stirring, until fragrant, 30 seconds.

Place the scallion whites and garlic, scallion greens, pumpkin seeds, and parsley in a food processor. Process until finely chopped. With the food processor running, slowly add the remaining ⅓ cup of oil through the feed tube. Process until combined. Add the vinegar, and pulse to combine. Season with salt.

PUMPKIN

swiss chard tabbouleh with pumpkin seeds

MAKES 4 SERVINGS

Rainbow chard adds bright pops of color to this classic Middle Eastern dish. The raw stems can be tough and fibrous, but finely chopping them helps combat this problem. Look for ground sumac (a tangy and tart spice) in specialty markets. If you can't track any down, substitute the same amount of finely grated lemon zest.

1 cup bulgur

½ bunch rainbow chard (about ½ pound), leaves finely chopped and stems thinly sliced

2 scallions, halved lengthwise and thinly sliced

½ cup toasted pumpkin seeds, chopped

¼ cup fresh mint leaves, chopped

¼ cup fresh lemon juice

3 tablespoons olive oil

1 teaspoon ground sumac

Kosher salt and freshly ground black pepper

Cook the bulgur according to the directions on the package. Drain and shake to remove as much water as possible. Spread the grains on a small baking sheet or plate and refrigerate, stirring once, until the grains are completely dry, 30 minutes.

Combine the bulgur, chard, scallions, pumpkin seeds, mint, lemon juice, oil, and sumac. Season with salt and pepper.

agrodolce sweet potatoes with creamy pumpkin spread

MAKES 4 SERVINGS

Tossing the sweet potatoes and tomatoes with vinegar (agro) and sugar (dolce) before roasting gives the finished dish pleasing sweet and sour notes. Served over a salty feta, toasted pumpkin seed, and fresh oregano spread, this is a standout summer-into-fall side dish that is great with roasted chicken or pork loin. The feta dip can be made up to one day ahead.

2 sweet potatoes (about 1½ pounds), sliced into ½-inch thick rounds

2 tablespoons red wine vinegar

1 tablespoons brown sugar

5 tablespoons olive oil, divided

Kosher salt and freshly ground black pepper

4 plum tomatoes, halved

1 sprig fresh oregano, plus 1 tablespoon leaves, chopped, plus leaves for garnish

4 ounces feta, crumbled (about 1 cup)

¼ cup toasted pumpkin seeds, coarsely chopped

Preheat oven to 375°F.

Toss together the sweet potatoes, vinegar, brown sugar, and 2 tablespoons of oil. Season with salt and pepper. Roast on a rimmed baking sheet, turning halfway through, until the sweet potatoes are tender, 30 to 35 minutes.

Toss together the tomatoes, oregano sprig, and 1 tablespoon of oil. Season with salt and pepper. Roast, cut-side up, on a separate baking sheet until soft, 25 to 30 minutes.

While the vegetables roast, make the feta spread. Combine the feta, pumpkin seeds, oregano leaves, and remaining 2 tablespoons of oil in a bowl. Season with salt and pepper.

Serve the sweet potato and tomatoes over the feta spread. Garnish with oregano leaves.

creamy cannellini bean soup
with spiced pumpkin seeds

MAKES 4 SERVINGS

Creamy soups are a must for the humdrum days of winter. They are warming and silky smooth, store beautifully (make a double batch and store it in the freezer), and are guaranteed to get you through those days when you just can't face the cold and a trip to the grocery store. Although rich, this soup is light on cream (only one-quarter cup) and bolstered by a sprinkle of spicy crunchy pumpkin seeds and a swirl of pumpkin seed oil on top. The soup can be refrigerated for up to five days or frozen for up to three months. The pumpkin seeds keep at room temperature for up to one week.

½ pound dried cannellini beans

3 tablespoons olive oil, divided

1 medium yellow onion, chopped

Kosher salt and freshly ground black pepper

4 cups vegetable stock (page 204)

2 sprigs fresh thyme, plus ½ teaspoon leaves

1 bay leaf

⅓ cup hulled pumpkin seeds

½ teaspoon red pepper flakes

¼ cup heavy cream

Pumpkin seed oil, for serving

TIP *If you have access to good-quality dried beans, like Rancho Gordo, opt for those. They have "best-by" dates on the packages, so you know how long they have been hanging around. Although they may be a bit more expensive, they are still cheaper than buying canned beans, and the consistent results and control make it worth spending a few extra pennies.*

Soak the beans in a large saucepan of cold water at least 12 hours. Drain.

Heat a large saucepan over medium heat for 30 seconds. Add 2 tablespoons of the oil and heat for 10 seconds. Add the onion. Season with salt and black pepper. Cook, stirring occasionally, until tender, 10 to 12 minutes. Add the beans, stock, thyme sprigs, and bay leaf. Bring to a boil. Reduce the heat and simmer, covered, until the beans are tender, 30 minutes to 1 hour.

While the beans cook, make the spicy pumpkin seeds. Place the pumpkin seeds, pepper flakes, and remaining tablespoon of oil in a small sauté pan. Cook over medium heat until the pumpkin seeds start to pop and become fragrant, 3 to 4 minutes. Remove from the heat. Add the thyme leaves and stir to combine. Season with salt. Drain on a paper-towel-lined plate.

Purée the soup, in batches, in a blender, until very smooth. Return to the pot and stir in the cream. Season with salt and pepper.

Serve the soup topped with the spicy pumpkin seeds and drizzled with pumpkin seed oil.

sweet and savory winter salad

MAKES 4 SERVINGS

When paired with spicy watercress, rich aged goat cheese, and speck, your boring typical fruit salad becomes fresh and modern. Speck is very similar to prosciutto but cured with spices and smoked in the final stage of curing, so it offers a more potent flavor.

1 bunch watercress, thick stems discarded

1 cup sliced red grapes

2 ounces speck, torn

⅓ cup toasted hulled pumpkin seeds

2 tablespoons olive oil

4 teaspoons white wine vinegar

2 ounces aged goat cheese

Kosher salt and freshly ground black pepper

Toss together the watercress, grapes, speck, pumpkin seeds, oil, and vinegar. Crumble the goat cheese on top and gently toss. Season with salt and pepper.

cauliflower and potato curry

Smooth tomato sauce sets the base for this restorative vegetarian curry. Garam masala, a mix of Indian spices, translated literally as "warm spice mix," is often made up of cinnamon, cloves, nutmeg, cardamom, peppercorns, mace, cumin, and coriander. Contrary to its name, however, the mix isn't spicy. Rather, the spice heats up the body by raising the metabolism. Serve the curry over rice with a few cilantro leaves for a fresh green hit and lemon wedges for a bright finish.

1 small yellow onion, chopped

1 pound red tomatoes, chopped

4 garlic cloves, chopped

1-inch piece fresh ginger, peeled and finely grated

2 tablespoons olive oil

2 tablespoons garam masala

2 teaspoons turmeric

2 teaspoons ground coriander

1 teaspoon black mustard seeds

1 small head cauliflower, cut into florets

½ pound Yukon gold potatoes, cut into ¾-inch pieces

¼ cup toasted pumpkin seeds

½ cup plain yogurt, plus more for serving

Cooked rice, lemon wedges, and fresh cilantro leaves and tender stems, for serving

Place the onion, tomatoes, garlic, and ginger in a blender. Process until finely chopped.

Heat a large saucepan over medium heat for 30 seconds. Add the oil and heat for 10 seconds. Add the onion mixture, garam masala, turmeric, coriander, and mustard seeds. Cook, stirring frequently, until darkened and very thick, 45 to 50 minutes.

Add the cauliflower, potatoes, pumpkin seeds, and 1 cup of water. Bring to a simmer and cook, partially covered and stirring occasionally, until the cauliflower and potatoes are tender, 12 to 14 minutes. Stir in the yogurt.

Serve over rice with additional yogurt, lemon wedges, and cilantro.

sausage and squash stew

MAKES 4 SERVINGS

Chorizo is a great shortcut ingredient. It is heavily spiced (paprika, coriander, and cumin, just to name a few) so you don't have to buy a lot of pricey spices to make this full-flavored stew. Here its flavors are complemented with chunks of creamy squash and wedges of sweet apples. Look for kabocha at farmers' markets in the late summer and fall. If it's unavailable, substitute acorn squash. The stew can be made up to three days in advance; store in an airtight container, in the refrigerator.

1 tablespoon olive oil

4 links fresh chorizo sausage

½ yellow onion, sliced

1 garlic clove, sliced

Kosher salt and freshly ground
   black pepper

¾ cup dry white wine (such as
   sauvignon blanc)

1 tablespoon all-purpose flour

2½ cups chicken stock (page 203)

1½ pounds kabocha squash, seeds
   discarded and cut into 1½-inch
   pieces

1 Pink Lady apple, cored and quartered

½ stick cinnamon

½ pound red cabbage, sliced

¼ cup Spiced Pumpkin Seed Shake
   (page 183)

Heat a Dutch oven over medium-high heat for 30 seconds. Add the oil and heat for 10 seconds. Add the chorizo. Cook, turning occasionally, until brown on all sides, 6 to 8 minutes. Transfer to a plate.

Add the onion and garlic to the pot. Season with salt and pepper. Cook, stirring frequently, until the onion is soft, 4 to 6 minutes (add a little water to the pot if the bottom becomes really dark). Add the wine. Cook until thick and syrupy, 5 to 6 minutes. Add the flour. Cook, whisking, 30 seconds. Slowly whisk in the stock. Add the squash, apple, and cinnamon stick. Season with salt and pepper.

Bring to a boil. Partially cover, reduce the heat, and simmer until the squash is starting to soften, 5 to 7 minutes. Add the cabbage and sausage. Cook until the squash and cabbage are tender and sausage is cooked through, 7 to 9 minutes.

Serve topped with the shake.

> **TIP** If you can't find fresh chorizo, it's OK to use cured, but it will need to be cut into thick chunks before browning. Remove from the pot as instructed, but don't return it to the pot until the vegetables are soft.

creamy chicken and pumpkin seed enchiladas

MAKES 4 SERVINGS

These enchiladas are mild and family friendly, but if making for children who are the slightest bit spice averse, simply leave out the jalapeño. Be sure to serve the enchiladas as soon as they come out of the oven when the creamy sauce will be at its best and the chicken is warm and tender. The sauce yields more than you'll need for the enchiladas. Serve the extra alongside the enchiladas or use it as a dip with tortilla chips.

2 small boneless, skinless chicken breasts (¾ pound)

½ pound tomatillos, chopped

1 cup toasted hulled pumpkin seeds

1 small white onion, chopped

2 cups fresh cilantro leaves and tender stems

1 cup chopped romaine leaves

3 garlic cloves

1 jalapeño pepper, halved

2 teaspoons dried oregano

1½ teaspoons ground cumin

3 tablespoons olive oil

2 cups chicken stock (page 203)

Kosher salt

8 corn tortillas, warmed

6 ounces pepper jack, grated, divided

Crema or sour cream, queso fresco, and lime wedges, for serving

> **TIP** *To heat the tortillas, roll them in a damp paper towel then microwave for 45 seconds. This will make them pliable and prevent them from cracking.*

Place the chicken in a straight-sided sauté pan and cover with water. Bring to a simmer. Reduce to a low simmer and cook until the chicken is cooked through, 15 to 18 minutes. Transfer to a plate. Shred with 2 forks.

Place the tomatillos, pumpkin seeds, onion, cilantro, romaine, garlic, jalapeño, oregano, cumin, and ½ cup of water in a blender. Process until smooth.

Heat a large saucepan over medium-high heat for 30 seconds. Add the oil and heat for 10 seconds. Add the tomatillo mixture. Cook, stirring often, until thickened, 10 to 12 minutes. Add the stock and cook until thickened slightly, 14 to 16 minutes. Season with salt.

Preheat oven to 350°F.

Spread 1 cup of the sauce in the bottom of a 3-quart baking dish. Place ½ cup of the sauce in a shallow bowl. Preparing one enchilada at a time, dip a tortilla in the sauce in the bowl. Fill with ¼ cup shredded chicken and 2 tablespoons cheese. Roll up the tortilla and place it seam-side down in the baking dish. Repeat with the remaining tortillas, chicken, and cheese. Top the enchiladas with the remaining ½ cup of cheese.

Cover the baking pan with foil and bake until the sauce is bubbling, 16 to 18 minutes.

Serve topped with *crema* and *queso fresco*, with lime wedges for squeezing.

arctic char and broccolini with pumpkin seed and lime sauce

A member of the salmon family, arctic char is a pink-fleshed fish (it's similar in color to salmon) with a light and delicate texture. It is available both wild and farmed, and either choice is preferable to farmed salmon. Because everything cooks on one tray, this dinner is easy to throw together. But don't let that make you think it's only appropriate for a weeknight family supper; the beautiful colors make for a spectacular, guest-worthy presentation.

2 bunches broccolini, trimmed and halved if thick

3 tablespoons olive oil, divided

Kosher salt and freshly ground black pepper

4 6-ounce arctic char fillets

Pumpkin Seed, Dill, and Lime Sauce (page 182)

Preheat oven to 400°F. Toss the broccolini with 2 tablespoons of oil. Season with salt and pepper. Roast on a rimmed baking sheet, tossing once, until crisp tender, 12 to 14 minutes.

While the broccolini is roasting, sear the char. Heat the remaining tablespoon of oil in a large non-stick sauté pan over medium-high heat. Season the char with salt and pepper. Cook, presentation-side down, until golden-brown, 5 to 6 minutes. Flip and cook until there is just the slightest bit of pink in the middle, about 1 minute.

Serve with the broccolini and topped with the sauce.

gingery pumpkin cheesecake

This very light and airy cheesecake is paired with a rich dark chocolate and pumpkin seed crust. The sour cream topping not only adds an amazing tangy flavor, it helps cover up any cracks that may form when the cheesecake is baking and cooling. Releasing the spring on the pan before the cheesecake has had much time to cool allows the crust to shrink along with the cheesecake and helps prevent large cracks. Store loosely wrapped, in the refrigerator, for up to five days.

24 chocolate wafer cookies

1¼ cups toasted hulled pumpkin seeds

¼ cup packed light-brown sugar

Kosher salt

6 tablespoons unsalted butter, melted

2 8-ounce packages cream cheese, at room temperature

¾ cup plus 2 tablespoons granulated sugar, divided

¾ cup pure pumpkin purée

1 teaspoon pumpkin pie spice

2 tablespoons plus 1 cup sour cream, at room temperature, divided

2 large eggs, at room temperature

Preheat oven to 350°F.

Place the cookies and pumpkin seeds in a food processor. Process until finely ground. Add the brown sugar and ½ teaspoon of salt. Pulse to combine. Add the butter. Process until the mixture comes together. Press the crust into the bottom and three quarters of the way up the sides of a 9-inch springform pan. Place on a rimmed baking sheet.

Beat the cream cheese and ¾ cup of granulated sugar with an electric mixer until light, 1 to 2 minutes. Add the pumpkin purée, pumpkin pie spice, 2 tablespoons of sour cream, and ½ teaspoon of salt. Beat to combine. Add the eggs, one at a time, beating well between each addition to fully incorporate. Pour the mixture into the crust.

Bake until the cheesecake has set around the edges but is still slightly wobbly in the center, 55 to 65 minutes.

Combine the remaining 2 tablespoons of sugar and 1 cup of sour cream in a bowl. Spread over the cheesecake, leaving a ½-inch border. Cook until set, 4 to 6 minutes.

Allow the cheesecake to cool for 5 minutes. Slowly release the spring on the pan to release the crust. Cool to room temperature then chill completely.

pumpkin seed brittle

MAKES 4 TO 6 SERVINGS

To get the perfect golden color and crunchy texture, you will need a candy or oil thermometer to make this brittle. Soft crack and hard crack indicate what the texture of the sugar syrup will be when cooled. For example, if you stop cooking the syrup when it reaches the soft-crack temperature, once cooled it will be soft and pliable. Try a bit of this salty sweet confection crumbled over vanilla ice cream or grilled fruit. Store in an airtight container, at room temperature, for one week.

2 tablespoons unsalted butter, plus more for the pan

1 cup sugar

⅓ cup light corn syrup

¾ cup hulled pumpkin seeds

¼ cup sesame seeds

1 teaspoon kosher salt

½ teaspoon baking soda

¼ teaspoon pure vanilla extract

Flaky sea salt (such as Maldon), for garnish

Generously butter a rimmed baking sheet. Combine the sugar, corn syrup, and ¼ cup of water in a medium saucepan. Cook over medium heat, stirring, until the sugar is dissolved and the liquid is clear. Increase heat to medium high and clip a candy thermometer to the side of the pan. Cook, without stirring, until the mixture reaches soft-crack temperature (290°F), 8 to 10 minutes. Add the pumpkin seeds, sesame seeds, butter, and kosher salt. Cook until it reaches hard-crack temperature (305°F), 1 to 2 minutes. Remove from the heat and stir in the baking soda and vanilla.

Spread the mixture on the buttered pan. Sprinkle with sea salt. Cool completely.

Use a small offset spatula or butter knife to release the brittle from the pan. Break into pieces.

cinnamon vanilla horchata

MAKES 3½ CUPS

Creamy yet dairy free! Horchata is typically made with almonds, but this version uses pumpkin seeds with cinnamon and vanilla added for spice. Feel free to adjust the sweetness to your liking, and if using sweetened rice milk, reduce the amount of sugar to one-quarter cup. Store in an airtight container, in the refrigerator, for up to three days, and add a splash of rum for fun!

1 cup short-grain white rice

½ cup hulled pumpkin seeds

½ cup sugar

1 stick cinnamon

1 vanilla bean, split lengthwise

1 cup unsweetened rice milk, chilled

Place the rice and pumpkin seeds in a blender. Process until very finely chopped. Add the sugar and 3 cups of warm water and process until combined. Add the cinnamon and vanilla. Chill at least 12 hours.

Strain the horchata through a fine mesh sieve. Stir in the rice milk.

Serve over ice.

Over and over, I find myself reaching for the following small batch of recipes. They are simple to prepare and work as a perfect base for many recipes in the book. While store-bought versions of all of them can be had, and I won't tell you to never to take a shortcut (I understand being busy!), these homemade versions are far superior. The flavors are cleaner and fresher, and in most cases, it is much cheaper to make these staples than to buy them.

STAPLES

pizza dough

MAKES 2 POUNDS

This simple dough requires no special equipment to prepare, only a little bit of time. If you are making it on a particularly cold day, let the dough rise a little longer than instructed. Store, tightly wrapped in plastic, in the freezer, for up to one month.

3 cups all-purpose flour, spooned and leveled, plus more for the work surface

1 cup white whole wheat flour, spooned and leveled

1 tablespoon kosher salt

¼ cup plus 1 tablespoon olive oil, divided

1½ cups water, warmed to 100 to 110°F

2 tablespoons sugar

2 packages fast active dry yeast (¼ ounce each)

Whisk together the flours and salt in a bowl. Rub the inside of a separate bowl with 1 tablespoon of the oil.

Combine the water and sugar in a measuring cup. Sprinkle the yeast on top of the water. Let sit until the yeast is bubbling, 5 to 7 minutes (if the yeast does not bubble, discard the mixture and start again). Whisk in the remaining ¼ cup of oil.

Add the wet ingredients to the dry ingredients and stir to combine. Transfer the dough to the oiled bowl and turn to coat with the oil. Cover the bowl with a dishtowel and place it in a warm (but not hot) place. Let the dough rise until doubled in size, 45 minutes to 1 hour.

Turn the dough out onto a floured work surface. Knead the dough until uniform, 8 to 10 times. Cover with the dishtowel and let rest for 5 minutes. Use as instructed.

chicken stock

Historically, stock is made with the by-product parts of a butchered bird—necks, backs, and carcasses. Since most grocery stores no longer have butchers (chicken parts are shipped to stores in bulk for repackaging), these parts are now hard to come by. Hence, chicken wing stock. Wings are cheap, easy to find, and full of great chicken flavor. In general, stocks are very forgiving, so if you have extra bones, from either a roasted chicken or butchering you did at home, feel free to substitute those for some of the wings. And don't bother peeling the carrots or onion (onion skin adds a nice color to the stock) or chopping any of the vegetables. Store in an airtight container, in the refrigerator, for five days, or freeze for three months.

4 pounds chicken wings

2 carrots

2 stalks celery

1 yellow onion, halved

2 sprigs fresh Italian parsley

1 bay leaf

1 teaspoon black peppercorns

Combine the wings, carrots, celery, onion, parsley, bay leaf, peppercorns, and 20 cups of water in a large stockpot. Bring to a boil then reduce to a simmer, skimming off any foam, fat, or brown bits, for 2½ to 3 hours.

Strain the stock through a double layer of cheesecloth or a dishtowel. Cool to room temperature then chill completely in the refrigerator.

Skim off any fat from the top of the chilled stock.

> **TIP** *If your freezer is too crowded for quart-sized containers, put the stock into large zip-top bags, about 4 cups per bag, squeezing out as much air as possible and freezing them flat. Once they are completely frozen, slide the bags into the freezer, upright like books on a shelf.*

vegetable stock

MAKES 10 TO 11 CUPS

As with chicken stock, vegetable stock is very forgiving and can be made with virtually any leftover vegetables. It's best to avoid loads of broccoli and cauliflower, though, because they will make the stock a bit odorous. Store in an airtight container, in the refrigerator, for five days, or freeze for three months (see chicken stock recipe, page 203, for a space-saving storage tip).

2 tablespoons olive oil

2 carrots, halved

2 stalks celery, halved

1 small fennel bulb, halved

1 yellow onion, quartered

4 garlic cloves, smashed

8 ounces cremini mushrooms

2 sprigs fresh Italian parsley

1 bay leaf

1 teaspoon black peppercorns

Heat a large stockpot over medium-high heat for 30 seconds. Add the oil and heat for 10 seconds. Add the carrots, celery, fennel, onion, garlic, mushrooms, parsley, bay leaf, and peppercorns. Cook, stirring occasionally, until the vegetables are brown, 8 to 10 minutes.

Add 16 cups water. Bring to a boil then reduce to a simmer. Simmer for 1 to 1½ hours.

Strain the stock through a double layer of cheesecloth or a dishtowel. Cool to room temperature then chill completely in the refrigerator.

ponzu

MAKES ½ CUP

This is a good all-purpose light and savory sauce. We use it a lot in our house when we are having our "we only have five minutes to make dinner" meal—steamed dumplings. Stir in canola oil and a few chopped scallions to turn it into a quick salad dressing. Store in an airtight container, in the refrigerator, for two weeks.

¼ cup mirin

¼ cup soy sauce

2 tablespoons fresh lemon juice

1 2-inch piece kombu (rinsed)

Gently simmer the mirin in a small saucepan until the alcohol is cooked off, 2 to 3 minutes. Add the soy sauce, lemon juice, and kombu and stir to combine. Let sit 10 minutes. Discard the kombu. Cool to room temperature.

harissa

MAKES 1¼ CUPS

The flavor of this tomato-based sauce is incredibly complex: It has heat, the tiniest bit of sweetness from the orange, lots of deep spice flavor, and a nice balance of acidity. Use it in place of ketchup on a burger or with fries, toss with roasted vegetables, or braise with Harissa Braised Chicken Legs (page 57). Store in an airtight container, in the refrigerator, for one month.

2 plum tomatoes

1 red bell pepper

1 tablespoon fennel seeds

1 teaspoon cumin seeds

2 whole cloves

2 garlic cloves

3 tablespoons fresh orange juice

2 tablespoons smoked paprika

2 tablespoons red pepper flakes

1 tablespoon sherry vinegar

1 tablespoon tomato paste

Kosher salt

Roast the tomatoes and bell pepper directly over two burners of a gas stove, set to high, or under a broiler, turning often, until black all over, 8 to 10 minutes. Transfer to a bowl, cover with a piece of foil, and allow to cool completely. Once cool, discard the blackened skin of both, plus the seeds and stem of the pepper.

Toast the fennel seeds, cumin seeds, and cloves in a small sauté pan over low heat until fragrant, 1 to 2 minutes. Finely grind in a spice grinder.

Place the peeled tomatoes and pepper, ground spices, garlic, orange juice, paprika, pepper flakes, vinegar, and tomato paste in a food processor. Process until almost smooth, 30 seconds to 1 minute. Season with salt.

METRIC CONVERSIONS

The recipes in this book have not been tested with metric measurements, so some variations might occur.

Remember that the weight of dry ingredients varies according to the volume or density factor: 1 cup of flour weighs far less than 1 cup of sugar, and 1 tablespoon doesn't necessarily hold 3 teaspoons.

GENERAL FORMULA FOR METRIC CONVERSION

Ounces to grams	multiply ounces by 28.35
Grams to ounces	multiply ounces by 0.035
Pounds to grams	multiply pounds by 453.5
Pounds to kilograms	multiply pounds by 0.45
Cups to liters	multiply cups by 0.24
Fahrenheit to Celsius	subtract 32 from Fahrenheit temperature, multiply by 5, divide by 9
Celsius to Fahrenheit	multiply Celsius temperature by 9, divide by 5, add 32

VOLUME (LIQUID) MEASUREMENTS

1 teaspoon = 1/6 fluid ounce = 5 milliliters

1 tablespoon = ½ fluid ounce = 15 milliliters

2 tablespoons = 1 fluid ounce = 30 milliliters

¼ cup = 2 fluid ounces = 60 milliliters

⅓ cup = 2 ⅔ fluid ounces = 79 milliliters

½ cup = 4 fluid ounces = 118 milliliters

1 cup or ½ pint = 8 fluid ounces = 250 milliliters

2 cups or 1 pint = 16 fluid ounces = 500 milliliters

4 cups or 1 quart = 32 fluid ounces = 1,000 milliliters

1 gallon = 4 liters

VOLUME (DRY) MEASUREMENTS

¼ teaspoon = 1 milliliter

½ teaspoon = 2 milliliters

¾ teaspoon = 4 milliliters

1 teaspoon = 5 milliliters

1 tablespoon = 15 milliliters

¼ cup = 59 milliliters

⅓ cup = 79 milliliters

½ cup = 118 milliliters

⅔ cup = 158 milliliters

¾ cup = 177 milliliters

1 cup = 225 milliliters

4 cups or 1 quart = 1 liter

½ gallon = 2 liters

1 gallon = 4 liters

WEIGHT (MASS) MEASUREMENTS

1 ounce = 30 grams

2 ounces = 55 grams

3 ounces = 85 grams

4 ounces = ¼ pound = 125 grams

8 ounces = ½ pound = 240 grams

12 ounces = ¾ pound = 375 grams

16 ounces = 1 pound = 454 grams

LINEAR MEASUREMENTS

½ in = 1 ½ cm

1 inch = 2 ½ cm

6 inches = 15 cm

8 inches = 20 cm

10 inches = 25 cm

12 inches = 30 cm

20 inches = 50 cm

OVEN TEMPERATURE EQUIVALENTS, FAHRENHEIT (F) AND CELSIUS (C)

100°F = 38°C

200°F = 95°C

250°F = 120°C

300°F = 150°C

350°F = 180°C

400°F = 205°C

450°F = 230° C

ACKNOWLEDGMENTS

t takes a village to make a cookbook, thus there are so many amazing, supportive, and brave people (there was a lot of food to eat) I want to thank.

Arnold, thank you for dealing with my meltdowns (and the smoke alarm constantly going off) on all of those hot summer days, making a million runs to the grocery store to pick up ingredients, eating everything I put in front of you, and the beautiful photographs. You said I could do it, and I did. I love you!

Thank you, Anna Beckman, for the beautiful watercolor of seeds. You're a real good egg.

Gina Smith, thank you for helping me not look like a total dummy, for letting me take over your kitchen on multiple occasions, and for being the greatest friend ever! See you at Smalls soon.

Sharon Bowers my amazing agent, from the second we met, you encouraged and pushed me to think big. You are my number-one cheerleader. My editor, Renee Sedliar, your feedback is invaluable and your positivity contagious. I hope this is only the start of our working relationship. Claire Ivett, for putting a keen eye on my recipes and words to make sure it was all in tip-top shape. Cisca Schreefel for keeping me on track and giving me weekends to work on edits, Megan Jones for designing beautiful pages, Kate Mueller aka copyeditor extraordinaire, Katie McHugh-Malm for eagle-eyed proofreading, and Jean DeBarbieri to put it all together in a clear index. I have Alex Camlin to thank for the beautiful cover; it's so exciting to see my name in print!

Sarah Brecht, Monita Buckwald, Shayna Cohen, and Randy Mattox (aka mom) for testing recipes and making sure they are all in tip-top shape. Anna Hampton for your inestimable help during the shoot. Thanks for enduring our tiny kitchen, family drama, and old-lady cat. It would not have gotten done without you! Heather Meldrom for carrying props up five flights of stairs and a much-needed third set of eyes.

Lindsay Hunt, Lygeia Grace, Heath Goldman, Chris Morocco, Dawn Perry, Cyd McDowell, and Sarah Copeland. Thanks for letting me bounce a million ideas off of you. I miss working, eating, and laughing with all of you.

INDEX

Page references in *italics* indicate photographs.